Sippers and Gulpers

Sippers and Gulpers

Gordon Turner

ISIS
LARGE PRINT
Oxford

First published in Great Britain 2007
by
Bound Biographies

Published in Large Print 2009 by ISIS Publishing Ltd.,
7 Centremead, Osney Mead, Oxford OX2 0ES
by arrangement with
Bound Biographies

British Library Cataloguing in Publication Data
Turner, Gordon
    Sippers & gulpers. – Large print ed.
    (Isis reminiscence series)
    1. Turner, Gordon
    2. Sailors – Great Britain – Biography
    3. World War, 1939–1945 – Personal narratives, British
    4. World War, 1939–1945 – Naval operations, British
    5. Large type books
    I. Title
    940.5'45941'092

    ISBN 978–0–7531–9526–0 (hb)
    ISBN 978–0–7531–9527–7 (pb)

Printed and bound in Great Britain by
T. J. International Ltd., Padstow, Cornwall

To all those who served on the LSTs, to my mates in the LST and Landing Craft Association, and especially to my darling wife Jen without whom this book would not have been written.

Acknowledgements

With thanks to Beryl Coster who helped initially with the typing of this book, to Mike Oke for bringing it to fruition, and to Jen for her encouragement and her special contribution.

Contents

Early Days

I left school at the age of fourteen and I was a bit put out because several of my mates were going to carry on with their schooling at a grammar school until they were sixteen. I had taken the eleven plus exam but was borderline and was not accepted at the grammar school so I now had to start work full time. It wasn't until I was much older that I realised what this meant to my future.

My brother Dick was now a full-blown motor mechanic after serving a five-year apprenticeship at Skurray's Motors in Swindon. I was of course a little bit in awe of Dick, but as it cost £100 for Mum and Dad to apprentice him I thought there wouldn't be much hope for me — a hundred pounds was a lot of money in those days. To clear the air I ranted and raved until Dad promised to make an appointment with Mr Skurray to see if they could offer me some hope. After a few weeks Mr Skurray gave me an interview, which went very well because he promised both Dad and myself that when I was sixteen he would apprentice me as a motor mechanic. It was all very exciting but I was a bit downhearted at having to wait two years, and £100 was still a hell of a lot of money to find.

By now I was getting to know about engines and motors as they were called then. I read books and helped Dick when he worked on Uncle Fred's car, a Citroen, and later an Austin 12 (I think). Two years seemed a very long way ahead and I could hardly wait to get my hands greasy. I even had a miniature spark plug to pin on my coat.

Now I had to think about work full-time until I was sixteen. Before I left school I had the usual job in those days for young lads of delivering morning and evening papers. I didn't mind getting up early and the money helped, and when I left school Mr Brewer, who owned the paper shop, said I could work full-time. In addition to delivering, I could collect the paper money on Saturday mornings and also collect the evening papers from the paper printing works in Old Town, this being a round journey of about four miles. I had the use of a carrier bike — the kind with a small front wheel and a large front carrier — very unstable when carrying three large bundles of newspapers.

The print works was at the top of a steep hill and I remember one day I was on the way back and was "motoring" down the first part of the hill when the speed and the weight on the front wheel made me wobble. I hit the curb on a small island and went sprawling into the road — the evening papers spread everywhere like confetti. I hit my knees and head, but I was not really injured, just a little bit dazed. I was lying in the road when a very kind pedestrian bent over and gave me a "penny" ... he wanted to purchase an Evening Advertiser! He took his paper and walked away without even helping me up (this is a true story). Luckily the bike was not damaged so I sorted the papers and made it back to the shop.

The evening papers had to be marked with the house numbers and then it was onto the bike again for delivery. On my way out I took three chocolate sweets from a tin of Quality Street — Mr Brewer was OK about this because owing to the accident I didn't have time for tea. I got on my way and, riding no-hands, took the silver paper off, popping the chocolate toffee into my mouth. Lo and behold instead of chocolate it was a piece of wood. When I got back I found that they were all wooden sweets in the tin — made up for sales purposes. The laugh was on me this time.

By now I was getting fed up with the paper business and was forever reading the "jobs on offer" pages, but there appeared to be little work available for "just left school" lads. It was difficult, because I was waiting for my apprenticeship and so was only marking time.

After I had been working full-time for about two months I was offered a job of working all day in the shoe shop owned by Mr Brewer, and then Saturday morning to cycle to houses in the district, knocking on doors and asking if anyone in the house required shoes mending. This seemed to work out quite well. I called at lots of houses and most people were pleased with the service, as I would offer them a price list and then deliver the shoes when ready. I remember that the "shoe snob" and Mr Brewer were both very pleased with my effort and gave me a bonus now and again, for business had picked up really well.

After a few weeks Mr Brewer started to stay away from the shoe shop for several days on end, leaving me in charge. Me, a shop manager at fourteen years old! Things started to go very well so I asked my mate Eric Sainsbury (Eggy) to come and help when he felt like it. As he had passed for grammar school he had a long holiday. I remember when Easter came along we decorated the shop window with a tree branch, artificial grass and a few dozen daffodils, all discreetly dotted with new ladies' shoes and sandals — although I say it myself, it did look good. All went really well, I enjoyed the work and "playing shop managers", until one fateful morning when a curtain used for keeping out the draught blew against an electric fire and caught fire causing damage to the shop and some of the stock. Of course Mr Brewer was not happy and Mum and Dad thought it was not right that a lad of my age should take on the responsibility of the shop. We had, however, put out the fire without calling the fire brigade so "old Brewer" could not rant on too much.

Looking back, Eggy and I did have some fun in that shoe shop, like trying to keep straight faces when selling shoes to old gals who paid with "trading cheques", which we did not know a lot about. Some of the "ladies" had holes in the toes and heels of their stockings, which also took some effort to keep a straight face.

After this setback we thought it best if I left the newspaper and shoe shop "management" and tried my

4

luck at engineering. Not far from home was a factory that manufactured record players and record changing mechanisms. Garrard's were also world renowned for their clocks and various instruments. Now because of talk of the coming war Garrard's had started war work, making bomb carriers that fitted under the wings of the Western Lysander, a small spotter plane.

Within a week or so of resigning my shoe shop employment I started work in the new Aircraft Department, which I believe was known as the AE Shop. My job was to drill holes in small metal plates and rivet them together, making a small oblong box which held a release solenoid. The rivets were not "ship size" I hasten to add — my rivets were only about half an inch long and one sixteenth of an inch thick, and were riveted with a small hammer and punch.

There were about 25 girls or young ladies and six blokes working in the shop, which was warm and clean with a good atmosphere. About fifty percent of the girls were old hands at Garrard's, but the rest of us had been taken on for the coming war work. Sat next to me was a man about 35 years old, doing the same work. I can't remember his name, but I think it was Jack. We got on quite well and I told him I had a brass cornet from my Grandad and had hopes of playing in a dance band one day. He then told me that he played a trumpet in a local dance band but had to pack up owing to his health, and he wondered if I would be interested in buying it from him. This of course made me very interested because most of my old school mates were into jazz. My best mate, Eggy Sainsbury, had a clarinet, Ken Morgan played drums and Ivor Matthews played the Alto Sax so I really thought this was a good opening for me.

When I went home that day I was very excited and told Mum and Dad all about buying the trumpet. At first they were not very impressed — they both asked me where I thought they would get the money to buy the trumpet and also pay for lessons. Of course I had to promise I would help out with the money, adding ". . . and who knows, I may get on well and earn lots of money playing in a band!" Again I got my way and the next day I talked to Jack about the trumpet, asking about it and if I could see it. He offered to bring it around to our house so that all at home could see it. So there you are — within a few days Jack came round to our house with his trumpet and in a couple of hours I was the proud owner of a beautiful Besson B-flat silver trumpet with a leather case and two "mutes", costing £8. At this time I was only earning about ten shillings (50p) a week, giving most of this to Mum for my keep, so £8 was a lot of money.

Most of my spare time was now taken up with going to trumpet lessons twice a week — I think these cost two bob a time. I went to a Mr Billy Walker, who was very good. He played trumpet in a very busy six-piece dance band, playing every Saturday evening at Shrivenham Memorial Hall and sometimes two dances during the week at village halls. I got on very well with Billy Walker — a strict man of about 40 years — and within seven weeks he had me playing some easy tunes. Within six months he suggested that I should go with him to Shrivenham every Saturday evening, which would be good for my playing and good experience if I wanted to take up the trumpet seriously.

Of course I was over the moon. I had thought I was years away from playing in a dance band, let alone playing second trumpet with five serious pro musicians. In no time I settled down in the local dance band named the "Red Aces". Of course all this stood me in good stead with my mates, and it wasn't long before we banded together in a small jazz band and played at our youth club and school jamboree. Life now seemed very good. The added bonus was that playing in a dance band was a hit with the girls!

My new job at Garrard's was going well and I had managed to get into their under-eighteen football team and later into their cricket team. Garrard's was a very good company to work for, owning their own sports field together with changing room and showers, as well as a football stand, and pavilion for cricket spectators. I enjoyed my time at Garrard's for about one year until I received a letter from Skurray offering me work as a mechanic's help until I was sixteen when, if satisfactory, I would start my apprenticeship. Everything was now opening up for me — I was a semi-professional dance band trumpet player and also set to be a full-blown motor mechanic.

Things started to go wrong when the talk of war became more real. Three mechanics at Skurray's who were in the Army Reserves received their call-up papers. In no time at all brother Dick, Charlie Rummings and Peter Haines were lined up to see the management and were off to the Army before we knew what was happening. We were all shocked, especially Mum and Dad who had gone through it all before in 1914, and of course Grace who had been married to Dick for a few months and was only just settling in to their new house. Only a few days after this it was announced that Germany had invaded Poland. I remember I was at home on the Sunday morning repairing a puncture in the back tyre on my bike. Dad opened the back door and called out, "Gord, come in and listen to the news." It was 11 o'clock on 3rd September 1939. I was soon in the kitchen where the wireless was on. There was great excitement in the air and of course a feeling of sadness.

The sombre voice of Neville Chamberlain somehow got through to us all: "We are at war." Now what? Are we all going to be killed? Of course not, we'll wipe the floor with that chap Hitler and the lads will be home in no time. Perhaps! Dad stood in front of the wireless looking bewildered and said, "It's you boys I worry about. I only hope it's not such a mess as our lot was. Just think, it was only 21 years ago when that ended — a war to end wars — and now here we are at it again."

Dad had been in the mud-filled trenches of Ypres. During an attack, as Dad said, the man next to him "had a shell all to himself". He was blown to bits while Dad received wounds to his head and left arm. Dad was send back to Blighty, but after a few months he was back on the front line. It was no wonder that his reaction to news of this new war was somewhat different to mine.

Life now began to harden, and food was rationed within a few months. Air raid shelters were distributed to homes — one sort of shelter was the Anderson, which was sunk in the back yards, and the other sort, the Morrison shelter, was a table. We had the latter. This was a steel table about six foot long and three foot wide with heavy steel legs. The side and end openings were covered with heavy steel mesh, which could be removed (with difficulty) to let us get in or out. I know it sounds a bit crude for a shelter but I can assure you they saved thousands of lives.

Now that war had really been declared there was an energy about everybody. More and more Army work came into Skurray's and we all had to work harder. Army motor training courses were set up at work. Everything one should know to be a mechanic was covered: welding, electrics, gearbox repairs, steering, engines inside and out. As I was one of the younger boys working at Skurray's I had to join the Army course.

By now outside our "motor world" the war was not going well. 158,000 British troops had been sent to France. The British battleship *Royal Oak* was sunk in Scapa Flow, and the USA had declared neutrality but allowed Allies to buy armaments from them. Weeks turned into months and the war seemed to have reached a stalemate, with not much action anywhere. The air war was very quiet, although several air raids took place on London and the south coast ports. At this time it was called a "phoney war".

Band work with the Red Aces was going well and I was now being paid five shillings an hour — one pound for a four-hour dance. I used to think, "how good being paid to enjoy myself."

As 1940 progressed the war hotted up. Norway and Denmark were invaded, and a small British force was sent to help. However, not knowing how the Blitzkrieg worked they were soon overcome and very few came home. The bombing of British towns and cities continued every day and night, and London was blitzed nightly. Thousands of kids were evacuated to the country, some being sent to Swindon. The German Army still pushed on — Holland, Belgium and Greece surrendered. France, although being helped by the British Army, also surrendered leaving the British to fight their way back to the Channel coast. They ended up trapped on the beach of Dunkirk, leaving our small island with a lost and shattered army.

The blitz on our towns and cities became worse, day after day. We could see and hear Bristol being bombed, and one night we spent hours outside watching the German planes flying over to bomb Coventry — we could do nothing but just watch. We did have some bombing in Swindon on Graham Street, Rosebery Street, and York Road just behind our house. We were in the kitchen listening to the wireless. The siren had gone and about ten minutes later we could hear the "whee whee" of bombs rushing down and then "boom"! The whole house shook and rattled and the lights went out. We were all shocked and someone said, "Christ! That was near."

In about a half hour the "all clear" sounded so Eggy and I made sure everyone in the house was OK. His and my family were OK, but we could see fire shooting up in the air — about 14 houses were destroyed and about eight died that evening. Three houses in York Road were demolished and a gas main in the middle of the road was alight, the flames shooting about 20 feet in the air. The plane was going home and had jettisoned its load.

With all this bad news flooding the country the people became very angry and there was anguish for our trapped army in France. Of course it had to happen — Neville Chamberlain was sacked and a National Government was declared, with Churchill being our new leader. Winston Churchill made a wonderful speech and a new spirit seemed to enter everyone. Thousands of fishermen and pleasure seamen turned into heroes. Boats of all sizes crossed the Channel to Dunkirk, and with the help of the Royal Navy and the RAF brought home the best part of our army, 338,000 men. People were saved but all the equipment lost.

A couple of days after Dunkirk lots of survivors came into Swindon station and were then marched through the streets of Shrivenham to the Army and Navy military college. It was a Saturday morning and we noticed people were gathering at the side of the road. We of course waited to see what was coming, then we heard the cheering — thousands of soldiers in all states of dress and condition marching. They marched keeping their heads held high, some singing. Some had their arms in slings, some had bandages around their heads and limbs, and some had crutches or sticks. Most of them were covered in sand and mud, but none of them looked beaten like we expected. People from the houses brought out cups of tea and sandwiches, and of course cigarettes, and we patted them on their backs and shoulders as they marched by. Later that day I realised our band would be playing that evening at the Memorial Hall in Shrivenham. It looked as if we would have a night to remember.

At about seven o'clock that evening as we arrived near the dance hall, all the grass verges at the roadside were covered with ragged soldiers lying and sitting on the grass, and crowds of girls and women were gazing and talking to their heroes. All of the soldiers were let into the dance free of charge and the bar was open to all. I don't know if they had to pay for drinks — perhaps not! We all had a wonderful evening despite the gravity of the situation. No one got out of hand and it all ended up with one big singsong.

There is one incident which I remember with amusement. We had packed up and were going back to our cars. It was very late and dark when I noticed a soldier lying face down in the grass just off the road. I thought he looked in distress so I wandered over to him and caught hold of his shoulder. I asked, "You OK mate? Do you want any help?" It was then that I wanted the earth to open up, as I could now see a girl beneath him! I got out fast, hoping no harm had been done — I didn't even say sorry!

After all the worrying news it was obvious that Britain was now on her own to save this island. Soon after taking charge, Churchill announced that a new force was to be formed made up of young and older men to guard vulnerable points and bridges, etc. if and when a German invasion came. All the volunteers would be issued with a uniform and arms when required but, owing to shortages, for the time being armbands marked "LDV" would be worn. When uniforms were issued, the Local Defence Volunteer changed its name to "Home Guard". Of course us "boys" were very excited with this news. At sixteen we could now do something to help the war and train to be soldiers. I was getting tied up with lots of things to do, what with band work twice a week, motor engineering night school two evenings a week and now Home Guard at least twice a week. Looking back, it appeared we didn't have time to be teenagers.

The Home Guard was good for morale. We went through drill called "square bashing", using broom handles instead of rifles. We practised manoeuvres in the local fields and then went on guard all night (four hours on, four hours off) at least one or two nights a week. Dad also joined the Home Guard; he was in a group based at the County Ground Hotel much to the amusement of Mum — as this, of course, was his local pub!

Together with a couple of my mates, Eggy Sainsbury and Colin Dolson, I enlisted into the Home Guard, our headquarters being the Gas Board Social Club, Gorse Hill, Swindon. The clubhouse was a good-sized wooden building adjacent to the cricket ground. At the front of the building was a narrow road named Gypsy Lane; at the rear were fields and hedges — just the job for square bashing and playing war games. About a mile from the clubhouse was an old disused munitions factory. This was a very large building with two very high brick chimneys, which could be seen from miles away. The building was derelict, with no doors or windows, and several inside walls had collapsed. The whole place was dangerous and should have been knocked down years ago. At night in the moonlight the whole building looked like a haunted castle.

The first guard duty for Eggy and me was to patrol the building inside and out to make sure no Germans were hiding. We were issued with one Royal Enfield rifle between us . . . and two bullets. We tossed up who carried the rifle. We were two seventeen-year-old youths creeping around this building, both frightened to death, never having fired a rifle in our lives. No Germans were found that night . . . and no courting couples rooted out — I wondered afterwards if this was a joke!

The next week I was detailed to guard Gypsy Lane bridge. This was a rail bridge over a single line, taking bunker trains to a halt just outside Swindon. I was on duty from six o'clock to eight o'clock in the morning. My duty was to stop everyone crossing the bridge and examine their identity cards. At that time of the morning lots of men were going to work on their bikes or walking. You can imagine what the men thought of a couple of kids like us stopping them with a rifle and demanding to see their ID cards. They must have though we were mad — we never did catch a spy or an invader!

Of course the Home Guard was new and training had not really started, but within a few weeks we all began to smarten up and feel better about ourselves, and I believe it did help the war effort. If the invasion did materialise we all had our orders what to do. All the church bells in Britain, which had been silent since the war started, would be rung letting everyone know the worst had happened. This feeling of waiting for something to happen went on for weeks, but eventually after watching our Spitfires and Hurricanes splitting up the German Luftwaffe and shooting them down, we began to feel all was not lost.

There was some good news coming in now and us boys began to feel we ought to be in the real service and were just waiting for the chance to make a move. By now I had met Jennie. Her looks knocked me over — her long dark hair and blue eyes were something. I used to see "Jen" when I was waiting for the car to turn up to take me to play at the dance on Saturday evening. She was usually with her mates messing about in the County Ground where we played football. I mentioned to Ken Morgan about her and he said that he fancied her too!

The next week I went roller-skating with some of the lads, during which, unfortunately, I knocked Jen over. I must have been ogling some other girl, not realising that Jen was even at the rink. I picked her up off the floor, very red-faced, and helped her to her seat. Of course that broke the ice and we started talking after I had apologised. We then spent the evening together and at the end of the skating I asked if I could take her

15

home ... and where did she live? "Stratton St Margaret," she replied. Blimey! That was about three miles from the skating rink. It worked out OK, though, because there was a good bus service and the bus stopped outside her parents' house. We didn't make another date there and then but I did say that I would see her again at the County Ground.

The next time I met Ken I told him about taking Jen home and asked him if he would come to the pictures with us if I got him a date with Jen's friend, Barbara. He said OK, but added that he would rather take Jen. This of course was no go with me, but I suggested that we should toss a coin for who should take her ... perhaps we should have asked Jen! Thankfully I won the toss, and got in touch with Jen to arrange to take her to the Arcadia, asking if she could ask Barbara to go with Ken. It all worked out well and I turned up dressed in my new overcoat, a grey check with a tie belt. Wow!

When we took our seats I took off the coat and folded it carefully, placing it under the seat. Towards the end of the film the island caught fire. It was thrilling and very realistic ... in fact, as the fire was raging, we could actually smell smoke coming out around us. I looked at Jen, who was wiping her eyes, so I bent forward and pulled my coat to get a handkerchief from the pocket. As I brought my coat out from under the seat a shower of sparks shot up between my legs. Cripes! My lovely new coat was on fire. I pushed my way past the people next to me and stumbled into the aisle. I could see that part of the collar and one of the sleeves was nearly burnt away. It was then that the manager turned up with a bucket of water and proceeded to dunk my coat into the bucket. "Hey! That's my new coat." It didn't make any difference, he just went on dunking and my coat was soaking wet. Not only that, but we were asked to leave the cinema, which we did in disgrace.

As if this was not bad enough, it was snowing hard outside, and I had to escort Jen home with a dripping overcoat over my arm. Of course this was also a disaster because I couldn't buy another overcoat as we now needed wartime clothing coupons. Despite this fiasco Jennie and I started going out together.

Life was hectic and I found it very difficult to find time to get all my learning and work in, and now on top of it all I had started courting. I was still only seventeen going on eighteen but I somehow felt that I should be doing more and getting more involved with the war. At the rate it was going on now it would be years and years before we could think of the future. I felt that I should be in the real service otherwise I would always regret not going to do my bit like Dad had done the last time.

Brother Dick had just come home from the Eighth Army in the North African desert, Italy and Crete. It had been in my mind for months to join up, but what service? That was the question. The RAF might be OK, but I didn't have the education for flying duty and I didn't fancy spending years in the middle of a cold flying field. My next thought was "What about the Army?" Well, what about the Army! No thank you. I didn't fancy rushing about in muddy fields, trying to repair trucks and muddy tanks. I could stay at home working at Skurray's if I wanted to do that. I think my mind had been made up for months; the Navy would be for me. I had no doubts, if the Navy would have me. It was possible I would hate it, but that's a chance I would have to take — in any case, the uniform was better than the other services!

I didn't mention "joining up" to Jennie or Mum and Dad. I thought it best to keep my counsel until the time came. When I did mention joining up to Jennie she didn't "kick and scream". I think she must have realised that the time would come eventually. This was also the reaction from Mum and Dad, which was understandable for most of the lads of our age were itching to have a go, especially as the war was still going badly for us.

It wasn't long before I wrote to the Naval recruiting officer and soon received a reply, with papers to fill in and a letter giving me instructions to go to their recruiting office at Bristol for a medical and an interview with an Engineer Officer. Of course I had to inform Skurray's that I had made my mind up to enlist, and it seemed my interview at Bristol went well as I was accepted. Skurray's were very good about it and said that my job would be waiting for me if and when I got back, and my apprenticeship would carry on from where I left off. This of course would depend on the length of time, and also how old I would be when I left the service of the Navy; it also depended on the feelings of both parties.

I was now wondering how long I would have to wait, and in the meantime I tried to find out what sort of life I had signed on for. I read all the leaflets they gave me and spoke to a couple of blokes who had been in the Navy, managing to get some idea of what I had let myself in for. It was pointed out that if I enlisted as a motor mechanic (this was a new position for wartime) I would start as a "leading hand" wearing an anchor badge on the left sleeve; my next "lift up" would be as Petty Officer. Uniform would be a peaked cap and blue suit with brass buttons. The type of craft I would be sent to would depend on how I came out in my training and exams. It was possible I would end up on a motor torpedo boat or submarine. To a young boy who had spent the last two years with war news, bombing and watching aircraft, the excitement of really taking part could hardly be contained. It sounded a good, exciting life to me, but I can imagine why those close to me thought I must be mad having a good job in a reserved occupation and giving it all up for the Navy. I had a good family and a lovely girlfriend so I had a lot to leave behind to go into the unknown, but somehow I felt I couldn't live with myself if I didn't play my part in this war.

I had now taken the plunge and signed away my freedom for as long as it took. There would be days and even weeks when I would hate the life, but my feelings then were good and I was looking forward to every minute.

A Real Eye-Opener

The Navy must have wanted me in a hurry, for I only had to wait a few days before I received my call-up papers and a train warrant ordering me to report to HMS Victory, Gosport at 11.00 a.m. on 27th July 1942. I would also require a change of underclothes for it was possible it would be several days before I would be issued with a full kit.

I eventually arrived at Gosport via train and ferry. There were about thirty new recruits also waiting to report and we were met by a three-badge Petty Officer who introduced himself and said that we were to be split up into two groups. It turned out that the group I was put into was made up of motor mechanics and diesel stokers and we would be moved in a couple of days to Chatham Naval Base where we would be kitted out to go through Royal Navy training.

We were given dinner and supper and introduced to a canteen and temporary sleeping quarters. Of course, we all felt very deflated having to wait a couple more days before we could really start, and on top of it all we had to keep out of sight as we had no uniform and no living quarters we could call our own.

After two days we were transferred to Pembroke Barracks, Chatham in the back of Bedford trucks just like cattle. We had started off at about six o'clock in the morning and arrived in Chatham just in time to catch breakfast and a cup of stewed tea. The truck took us straight through the front gates and into the barracks where we disembarked and marched into the main administration building — a large barn-like structure next to the parade ground.

The first thing that happens when one joins a Royal Navy barracks anywhere in the world is to carry out "joining routine" and then be issued with a station card. This card is actually a breathing licence. Life as we knew it depended on the card. The card could be taken away by Chiefs and Petty Officers for even the slightest misdemeanour and to retrieve it was hell for new recruits, having to attend a morning court or "rattle". You would have to stand to attention in front of the Petty Officer and Officer of the Watch. "Off caps" would be barked at you, after which your crimes would be read out and then you had to try to explain why you had been a "naughty boy". If found guilty, the Officer would "weigh you off" by imposing your sentence, such as two days stoppage of leave, or maybe seven days or months, depending on the severity of the crime. For really serious cases, such as theft or thumping a PO, then the case would be adjourned to a higher naval court.

Pembroke Barracks was known for its discipline, with Chiefs and Petty Officers walking in pairs all over the place, even in the "heads" (toilets), all wearing black gaiters and black belts and looking like the Devil Incarnate, and their eyes looking everywhere hoping to find some poor sailor trying to hide out of their way. If you had to cross the parade ground, this had to be done "at the double" and it was even worse entering the gunnery school where everything was to be carried out "at the double". If you did step over the line and walk over the parade ground, a shrill whistle would pull you up straightaway — a black-gaitered Chief would put his face about an inch away from your face and growl "Give me!" That would be your breathing licence gone again!

The first day of joining routine included visiting the doctor, and visiting the uniform, kit, and bedding station — bedding included hammock and mattress. Each department we visited took time and we had to wait in queues until we had all gone through the whole routine. After visiting all the different departments and signing papers that were put in front of us, we were told to stow away our brand-new kit and go back to the clothing store for any alterations required. That day and part of the next day had now gone, so the next on the list was to be introduced to the Chief Petty Officer in charge of our training.

Seamanship was high on the list, even for the engineering department. For everyone who was going to war on ships seamanship included short lectures of reading flags and Morse code, rowing and swimming. The first lecture from our Chief, George Cox, was "the uniform and pride". He told us that we should have a gut feeling that the Royal Navy uniform is the greatest in the world, and he would come down like a load of bricks if he found anyone disgracing it. I think his lecture was great and it has stuck with me ever since. That's why I have marched with the Royal Navy in London, USA, and once in Paris — parading around the Arc d'Triomphe to the cheers of the locals.

This naval training continued for several weeks — marching, football, swimming, how to tie a hammock and also the use of naval language. In fact I think I enjoyed most of it. Every Sunday morning we had to attend the C. of E. church service and then a parade behind a full Royal Marine Band in dress uniform and white pith helmets — up and down the large parade ground (like kids!) not like men!

Pembroke Barracks was quite good once you got used to the discipline, but there was one thing I could never understand — why there were not enough bedrooms to go round as most of short-stay recruits had to sling their hammocks in the tunnels. There was quite a large warren of tunnels under the main barracks. I really don't know why the original tunnels were built, but they certainly were put to good use for the wartime influx of new recruits. Large ring bolts were fitted to the walls and roof so that hammocks could be slung in, row upon row. It was an amazing sight to see hundreds of hammocks with "dead to the world" sailors, some with their legs hanging over the sides of their hammocks, and most snoring — oblivious to the hundreds of men swinging alongside them.

I think I lost my station card for the first time in these tunnels. I had a very late night with four of the lads, playing cards and having a few beers, and it must have been about two o'clock in the morning when I slung my hammock. I was well away in "Noddy Land" when all of a sudden I felt a rough hand shaking my shoulder and a shout in my ear, "What the hell do you think you're doing? Give me your station card, sailor!" The Chief was doing his rounds at 10.00 o'clock in the morning. I sat up with difficulty and could see an empty tunnel where hundreds of hammocks should be swinging. Talk about a frightened kid. I thought the end of the world had come. I think I got my card back the next week — no harm done, but a very chastened kid for the next few days. Every time I saw a pair of black gaiters coming, I shuddered.

One of our training subjects was "Hammocks, for the Use of". The hammock was almost an icon in the Royal Navy at that time. We were told how to make up and then tie up the hammock, how to fit the clews and fix with special knots, and to roll it up for tidy stowing. The hammock had to be folded with blankets and clews inside. One end was "tied with the lashing" and the whole thing was rolled like a sausage and held together with the lashing rolled round with seven hitches. Pulled tight, this hammock would be very tidy when slung over one's shoulder. I believe the seven hitches was something to do with the seven seas, or so they told us and I believed them! I did manage to get the hang of it, but, when I eventually went to the yankie-made ship, bunks were now in fashion and all my hammock training was a waste of time.

Training was slipping by very fast and I started to go ashore with the lads. Even when living in a land-base barracks we had to use naval talk — going out of the barracks was "going ashore". Chatham was a small town just like Swindon — not a lot to do, but the pubs were great and there were several cinemas, and the barrack facilities were good.

I had now been in barracks for several months and was waiting for my first draft chit (ship or establishment), when I was handed a note from the Captain saying he wished to see me. Of course, this caused great concern, for no one had heard of this happening before, and I had to make an appointment through the chief of the depot. I eventually met the "great man". He told me that a dance band at Rochester Casino was looking for a trumpet player and as he had heard I played a trumpet and I had the trumpet with me, if they would agree, he would let me have leave to play for the band at weekends. What a "turn up"! Within a few days it was agreed that I would play for their Saturday dances for a fixed fee. I played for them for three weekends, before they eventually obtained a full-time player. I enjoyed the experience, but it couldn't go on for much longer; I had to get some leave in, because I expected to be drafted to a ship, or the next training department very soon.

I did manage to get seven days' leave and this time I wore my new suit — a tailor-made doe skin, double-breasted suit with gold badges — some difference from the single-breasted three-buttoned jacket that was issued. I wasn't very happy with that uniform, for we used to get mixed up with railway porters when we wore it near the train station.

The other gripe I had was the peaked cap that was issued. You could always tell an old hand by the shape of his cap. The front of the cap had to be pulled up in the front and held up with about an inch-and-a-half of a broken hacksaw blade; the back of the cap had to be pulled down and the whole thing worn at a slight angle — almost like a Nazi SS guard (may I say it). Anyway, after several months I did manage to get the cap right in my imagination! To prove this, I remember a few months into my service that we were being inspected by a "high up" officer. He stopped in front of me and looked with piercing eyes and barked, "Who the hell do you think you are? Admiral Bloody Beatty?" and then he screwed my cap straight on my head. I thought afterwards my cap must have looked good to make him as jealous as that!

I must say my leave went off very well, what with my new-tailored doe skin suit and my reassembled cap. After my leave, Jen and I parted, not knowing what was in front of us and how long it would be before I was home again, and of course, there were not many dry eyes around.

Back at Pembroke Barracks our first job each day was to look at the notice board to see who had a draft chitty posted. Then eventually the day came — I was drafted to Asbury Park, USA, to leave on an undisclosed date. Of course, there was a big buzz of excitement within our group — where is Asbury Park? When would we be going? Several days went by, every day bringing different stories, until the eventful day when we were told that we would be leaving Chatham for Southampton the following morning. We had to muster in the administration building with full kit and hammock at 0900 hrs, after carrying out "leaving routine". There were to be about 300 leaving that day, so we guessed it would be a big ship — it turned out to be a big ship, a very big ship — the Queen Mary. Of course, we newcomers were very excited. Going to the States on the Queen Mary!

Everything seemed to be moving on in a rush. There was packing of kit bags, making sure all our laundry was clean, letters to be written and no mention of the USA or that we were moving to pastures new. Until now I had not thought much about America, but I did wonder how they could stand by and watch the Germans bomb and shoot thousands in Europe. Since being bombed in Pearl Harbor in December 1941, they were pulled into the war, which of course took a lot of pressure off us, and no doubt it could all be over long before we thought.

The next day all those going on draft were ushered into a fleet of buses and we arrived at Southampton within a few hours. As we entered the dock, the great black liner could be seen at anchor in The Solent. We had to board her via a tender, and all the kit bags, hammocks and luggage went aboard by a working party, to be sorted out later. We were surprised to find that the service crew — that is, bag handlers, and stewards and service police — were personally supplied by the RAF.

Later in the day we all had to muster in certain areas and RAF guides gave us written instructions where our messing, sleeping and ablutions were situated in a maze of corridors and cabins. All the fine carved wood panels and luxury carpets had been removed or covered with plywood. With regards to the living quarters, cabins were fitted with bunks for sleeping, and of course several of the upper decks were left with cabins in normal conditions for the top brass.

There were also several large rooms which had no doubt been dance halls or special dining rooms in peacetime. They were now put aside for troop recreation, although no gambling was permitted. It was, however, noticed that Crown and Anchor, Housey Housey and Brag were always in full swing. It was known from the "underground" that gambling was run by "hard boys" and they had a gang of "eyes" who kept watch for the RAF police, who were on the lookout for heavy gambling and would no doubt close down all the entertainment. Some of the boys who were on the lookout were paid loads of money for staying awake every evening until the early hours of the morning. We never did hear if the gambling syndicates were broken.

We were on board for seven days, and as this was my first voyage I was enjoying it. The food was very good, all the American food I had seen in American films — cream cakes, hot dogs, hamburgers and, especially, sliced white bread. To us Brits this was the first time we had seen sliced bread. The coffee was also real, not like the rubbish we had been used to in the '30s. There was of course, no hard drink, only coffee and milk from coffee bars which always seemed crowded with American troops, so we began to wonder why the yanks were going home so soon — they had only joined our war a few months ago!

As we left Southampton there were plenty of ships of war anchored in The Solent, but we carried on to cross the "pond" without escorts. The Queen Mary could outrun any ship the enemy could send after us, having held the Blue Riband. As soon as we were at sea the whole complement of passengers was called to attend lifeboat drill. We had already been given a lifeboat number and were told to muster under that boat hanging from its davit. In our lifeboat group was an American Naval officer whom I thought I knew or recognised. I whispered to several around, "Who's that?" He turned out to be Douglas Fairbanks Jnr — the famous film star. I think he was put in charge of our lifeboat.

The days on board went very quickly and we were making good progress all through. There was a heavy swell which caused the great liner to lift to quite a height and return without a splash. In fact, it was smooth and one did not realise that the sea was rough. For myself, I was happy I was not ill or seasick as this was my first voyage. The only thing I noticed was feeling more tired than usual. I put this down to walking along the long corridors and stairways. The ship was rising and falling in the heavy sea — on the rise it felt like walking up a steep hill, but on the fall it felt like running downhill. Walking the corridors, you couldn't see the ocean, and the rise and fall was so slow

you could only feel the movement through your legs —
anyway, that was my theory! One moment you would
have short legs and the next you would have long legs
and start running. No wonder I felt tired.

At sea there was nothing happening to remind us we
were at war. The only excitement was sighting a whale
that came quite close, but suddenly turned and dived
waving his large tail, as if waving us goodbye. On the
fourth day, there was land ahead, Nova Scotia, and
several hours after that the coast of the USA could be
seen: Boston, Cape Cod and then Long Island, and
then the excitement of seeing the Statue of Liberty
come into view. I was a bit disappointed, for the statue
appeared a lot smaller than I had imagined.

By now, New York was well and truly in view — the
skyscrapers, bridges and waterways were just like
the picture postcards. It took a few hours to enter the
Hudson River and find our "parking lot" in New York
harbour. Our lot was right next to the remains of the
French Blue Riband liner, Normandie, lying on her
side — just a blackened shell. She had burnt out and
rolled onto her side a few years previously.

We were now secure, alongside, right in the heart of
New York, waiting to go ashore and taste the life of the
yanks. It was very late and we were informed that we
would be moving off the Queen Mary early the next
morning. We had to make sure our kit bags and
hammocks were all packed and no kit left behind. On
leaving the Queen Mary all the ratings would move into
temporary accommodation near the New York docks,
and then onward to Asbury Park, where two large

holiday hotels had been requisitioned by the US Navy to house the Brits who had been earmarked to sail the LST (Landing Ships Tank) and the smaller LCTs (Landing Craft Tank) that were being built all over America.

The LST was designed with the help of British draughtsmen and Winston Churchill, who stipulated what would be required to land two armies onto French soil. The cost, of course, would have to be borne by the British.

Within a few days all those who had left Chatham Barracks to man the landing craft and ships were bussed to Asbury Park and were soon settling into the two hotels. Both of these were modern and before the take-over had been clean, family holiday hotels. When the buildings were taken over by the Navy all the bedroom doors were taken off their hinges, all carpets removed, and most of the ratings had to sleep on their mattresses on the floor — in other words, "back to basics" in this rich country! Both of the hotels had been turned into a "make do" barracks and we were all issued with a "breathing licence", the station card.

In reality Asbury Park was a nice little holiday and college town, with plenty of watering holes and eating places — to us this was a bonus, for I think in those days my home town had about two restaurants, and only a few pubs served lunch other than a bag of Smiths crisps. We spent about three weeks in this town and I had shore leave every evening. Of course, we all belonged to two watches — Port and Starboard — and we took "turn about" every other day on duty . . .

except for me. I somehow got hold of two station cards, so I went ashore every evening without anyone wondering why!

There were several cinemas and a couple of dance halls, and of course plenty of bars, so we had enough entertainment to keep us happy for a few weeks. Everything was so different from home — the teenagers dressed colourfully without being bashful, and everyone talked loudly. Often we would be sat at a table in a café or bar and two or three young girls would come and sit beside us and drawl in yanky talk, "Say, hello boys! You just come all the way from little ol' England? Just talk to us, we love to hear the way you talk." And there we were, almost ashamed of our broad Wiltshire, Northern, Scottish and Cockney accents, but these girls loved it. Perhaps that's why I have never tried to lose my broad Wiltshire accent!

I remember once three of us "limeys" were taken to a high class night club and after dinner a series of older women (some almost like Dame Edna) came to our table and held our hands making us feel like ten-year-olds. They said something like this, "You poor young boys have come all this way from Britain. It must be terrible. Have you been starving? Were you frightened of those terrible bombs? Did your house get blown up?" etc. It was embarrassing at the time, but I think they meant well and plenty of drinks did follow them to our table.

We were getting to enjoy our time in Asbury, but in a couple of weeks we received our marching orders to Chicago. The destination was to be The Pier, Lake

Michigan, Chicago, and we were travelling in a couple of days by steam train. Once again everything was "go, go". A fleet of Army trucks turned up to collect our bags, hammocks and kit bags filled to the brim. They detailed about thirty of our draft to go with the trucks to New York to unload all the bags at the Grand Central Station. On the way back to our hotel there were numerous traffic lights, and every time the lights were red, two or three of the boys would slip over the tailgate and disappear into the nearest bar. Only about half of the baggage party returned to the hotel that night! As far as I know no one was put on a charge for skiving-off when on baggage party duty. As for me, I got away with it because I had an extra station card.

Early next morning the Chicago draft was transported to the Grand Central by buses, and on arrival we had to find our kit and hammocks and stow them away in large wagons at the end of the train standing at the station. On entering the Grand Central, the entrance and reception area made us stop and look up and around in awe — it was vast, more like going into a cathedral than into a dirty train station. The engine and carriages were large, like everything in the USA. All our sleeping cabins were booked and numbered and there were four bunks to each cabin. There was a good restaurant taking up the whole of one carriage and an observation carriage at the rear, and, yes, there was coffee on tap all day.

Crowds of passengers, private and Navy, were filling up quickly and most of the Navy boys were sticking together, except for one — he was not a boy, he was an engineer commander RN, who had been staggering around the station most of the morning. He had a half bottle of rum in his hand and sometimes in his mouth, and from his feet dragged his sock garters as he staggered along with the crowd. We were all very ashamed, a Royal Navy officer letting down his country and also the uniform of the Royal Navy. I bet that Chief Petty Officer who gave us our first lecture at Chatham Barracks would have thumped him if he was there. I don't know if that commander ever arrived in Chicago with us, but I never set eyes on him again.

The train journey took about two days and one night of life-lasting memories of good food in a first-class restaurant and wondrous views from the observation carriage. What a war for some! We sped through states, towns, cities with magical names like Pittsburgh, Pennsylvania and Indiana, to name but a few, sitting or lounging in the observation carriage sipping a glass or two of lager and staring at the different views that flashed by, or stayed still when we stopped at crossings or stations. In the '40s there were still plenty of prairies left and also groups of Indians, complete with their wigwams and ponies, still keeping the old legends alive. Where were the cowboys, I wondered? Perhaps some were the great-grandads, or grandads, of the bemedalled sailors, airmen and soldiers who had now reluctantly come to our aid. We swept through the outskirts of towns and cities and lots of very small hick towns with horses tethered outside shops and wooden drinking bars.

Once again, my memories of childhood began to run riot and I hoped to see a black-hatted baddy being thrown through the bar window or perhaps jumping off a veranda onto the back of a bronco. Of course, this was all wishful thinking, for in reality most of the small towns were very quiet, except for a horse and trap, or a monster Buick filled with colourful teenagers speeding along the dusty road. I think I saw more action on Home Guard duty in Swindon.

The day was now drawing to a close, and most of the RN boys were almost asleep, for this had been a very tiring and exciting day, what with starting very early having to load all the kit. It was a day that I wouldn't have missed, but we all thought it was time to get our heads down and try out the bunks in our cabins. I know I slept like a log and looked forward to the next day.

The journey through the night went well; it was a bit of a rock-and-roll experience according to some of the lads, but I didn't open my eyes until the clatter of cups woke me up at about 6 o'clock. Hot coffee and biscuits in my bunk, and later in the restaurant carriage after ablutions was my order of fried eggs and bacon (the full whack). Back into the observation carriage feeling my age (eighteen), we watched America slip by until we came to the outskirts of Chicago. The train slowed down, rumbling over the multitude of rails and points until we stopped with a jolt at Chicago's platform, the end of a great journey.

There were crowds of people milling about the platform, and we had to unload all our kit and load up the waiting Naval buses to take us to our quarters for the next few months, which happened to be on the pier on the waterfront of Chicago. The city was hundreds of miles inland set on the banks of Lake Michigan, just like a seaside town at home with a pier, which had been turned into a Naval establishment. The building was a Naval barracks three or four storeys high with the whole works — sleeping quarters, gymnasium, dance hall, shower rooms, bars, restaurants and lecture rooms. In fact, it was a full-blown naval barracks built on the lake and run by the US Navy.

The barracks housed all American Naval ratings, and the only group of British sailors was our group. We were there to learn the workings and the technical details of the American-built General Motors two-stroke diesel engines, two of these engines being fitted to the new LST landing ship — this being a large flat-bottomed ship to be used in an attempt to land US and British forces on the beaches of Europe. No doubt in a few weeks' time we should know all about these engines and also the new ships, LSTs, if we were going to sail back across the Atlantic to dear old beleaguered Britain.

The first night in the barracks was quite normal; the bunk beds were comfortable and the room was large — more like a hospital ward. I think there were about eight beds and lockers either side, making a passageway straight through between the ends of the beds, with a door at each end. The toilets and shower room were at the far end. We all slept like logs until about 6 o'clock, when we were fully awakened by a small-size brass band, including drums and trumpets, playing America the Brave, which marched straight through the bedroom just to impress us "limeys"! We found out afterwards this happened only about twice a month, thank goodness!

The next morning we were awoken slightly differently — a Chief Petty Officer stamped through shouting, "Wakey! Wakey! Hands off cocks, on socks!" I ask you! More like a comic opera than a Navy. I am not grumbling for we were treated very well and there was always a "full wax" hot breakfast every morning. After breakfast, we could join in with the home team for morning exercise if we wanted, but we did have to muster in our classroom for the start of our course with introductions to our instructors and also the GM V12-567 2-stroke diesel engines.

The course was very good and I really tried to learn as much as I could, for this time our lives depended on good old-fashioned "know how". Breaking down in the middle of an ocean with U-boats lurking is slightly different to breaking down on country roads back home — this was proven to me several times during my time in the Navy.

Our first day shore leave in Chicago was a real eye-opener for me. Outside the entrance to the pier, several large cars waited, some with chauffeurs at the wheel, while the owners were standing at the side of the pier to meet and talk to the Brits as we came ashore. I was with two of my "oppos" who I had teamed up with, so we were cornered by a tall, handsome, middle-aged man. He shook our hands and welcomed us to the USA, and then invited us to his home for a dinner party with his family that evening. Of course, we were taken aback, as we had been warned about going home with strange men by the US Navy top instructor. This man could see that we were reluctant to go off in his car, so explained he was the Mr Johnson of Johnson & Johnson baby powder fame. He was of English descent and he wished to show his appreciation for the British war effort. We had heard of Americans inviting British sailors home, but bearing in mind there were three of us and all fit, we could look after ourselves, so we thanked him for his kindness and agreed to be picked up at 8.00 o'clock that evening, outside the pier. So our first day ashore turned out to be great.

We had no idea where to go, or what to do, so the morning we spent gawping at all the new sights and clubs, and the bright shops and stores, which seemed to sell everything on earth, and then we decided to try the elevator. There was no underground railway, but instead there was an overhead railway that travelled on a rail loop right round the city, held up by towers about thirty feet high. It seemed to work like our underground, but instead of rushing through dark tunnels, you were transported above the smoking, crowded inner city. It was particularly exciting going over the playground area — the theatres and clubs, the lakeside cafés, shops and shows. No doubt these were the clubs and streets where legends of the gangsters and bootleggers began. I decided I would have some of this before I was shipped back to the real war zone. We spent the rest of the morning and afternoon wandering around the shops, eating and drinking as one does when trying to waste a few hours. Fed up of doing nothing, we returned to the pier and got our heads down for an hour or so.

By 6 o'clock it was time for a wash and brush up and to climb into my new No.1 uniform made of doe skin with gold buttons and gold badges and worn with a black bow tie, all ready for our dinner party date with the Johnson baby powder man and his family. Who knows, there might be a gangster's moll or two still hanging about?

Spot on 8 o'clock we went to the pier entrance and there was the chauffeur in the large Packard limo waiting to whisk us away to the grand party. We discussed the party when we walked around the city, and both Tom and his oppo John said there would be no harm in it. In one of the bars the barman had warned us about some men who were on the prowl for young servicemen like us, so we had to be careful. However, we need not have worried as it was a really lovely party. The house was grand with a large dining room with half-a-dozen or so waitresses making sure we all had plenty to eat and drink and wanting for nothing. The family were very nice, if a little bit over the top and gushing, like a lot of Americans. I thought we were a bit young for their sort of party. I was surprised with the food, for it was all "help yourself", with one large plate and fork. The plate would be piled up with all sorts of food — spicy meat and birds, with sweets and cakes all topped up with cream and trifle. Wow! At home we would have a clean plate for pudding . . . and we didn't have dishwashers! Drinks started to flow, all with names we had never heard of, so we just had to close our eyes and take a chance with the good old faithful gin, rum and whisky.

After dinner we met the family and guests, and talk always turned to the war and the bombing of the English cities. At this stage, we had seen nothing of the war, but they thought we were heroes, and the older women loved to hear us talk. It was about 11 o'clock when a 4-piece band arrived, which livened things up. Unfortunately, the time flew by, so at one o'clock we told Mr Baby Powder we should be getting back to our pier, as we had a war to fight — laughter all round. Mr and Mrs Johnson thanked us for turning up and wished us all the luck in the world and asked us about our Mums and Dads and family at home. We, of course, thanked them for their kind invitation and the lovely evening they had given us. I didn't say I would keep in touch as I thought I had a big job now trying to write to all at home and elsewhere. I have thought what may have happened in later years if I had kept in touch with them. Within a short time of small talk the limo was waiting in the front forecourt. "Cheerios" were again called and we were soon silently swishing through the outskirts of Chicago leaving the large millionaires' pads behind.

The lights of the city were still ablaze and patrons of the numerous private clubs, casinos, and bars were still entering, and some leaving, as most of these places were open all night. When we alighted from the warm limo we noticed how bitterly cold it was getting; in fact there was a slight fall of sleet or snow. Winter was approaching and Christmas was around the corner. Back on the pier, things were now starting to settle down.

Life was as good, as one would expect, and the LST course was excellent. Besides lectures and writing reams of engineering notes, we were working with the full engine, dismantling and rebuilding major parts. These engines were large V12 diesel two-stroke with uni injectors, which were each tuned individually. We were taught how to dismantle and rebuild injectors and pumps, which was completely new to me. I was forever thankful that I took it all in and did not waste my time by fooling around. I found out later the early LSTs were prone to breakdowns and that's not good if you are in the middle of the Atlantic in 1942 without a paddle, and no working knowledge of the engine.

We awoke a few days later to a white world of snow which had fallen the whole night and the deadly Chicago wind had set in. Poking my nose outside in the morning, it could be seen that the water on the lakeside was starting to freeze. The very cold wind was blowing and my eyes started to water from the intense cold, and then my eyes felt as though they had grit in them. The trouble was the tears in my eyes had started to turn to ice — not nice, but no worry, when I knew the cause. Better buy some eye muffs!

We spent about five weeks living on the pier, which was quite enjoyable for there was plenty to do in Chicago and we had every evening off. After the evening meal we were free until 7 o'clock the next morning. Of course, we didn't go out every evening for none of us was very flush with dollars; we all knew American servicemen were paid more than us.

The course was arranged to go on for another two weeks and then we would all go our different ways to join our new ships, now undergoing sea trials at their respective shipyards. We were approaching Christmas, so we were hoping we would still be in Chicago with the people we were beginning to know. A new ship with all new crew would be a damp squib for a good Christmas. The weather was now all white and the whole city seemed to be full of Santa Clauses of all sizes, some fat and red-faced and others skinny — like Al Capone, waiting to waylay the children.

During this time, there was another group of LST engine room engineers waiting to arrive and take ourusb places on the pier, so about ten of us had to move out and go into private digs. I was allocated to a three-storey house with basement in a long street of attached houses. It was a clean area of working-class families, and they soon made me welcome. The family consisted of Mum, Caroline, and Dad, Greg, a 12-year-old son, Adam, and a 17-year-old daughter Sammy. They were a nice family and made me very welcome, but I did feel a bit strange not having any of my "oppos" staying with me. It was only for two weeks, so I had to put up with a happy home.

I went out a couple of evenings to a nightclub with Carol and Greg. It was called The Trilby, a well-known night club where big bands played real jazz — just up my street. I did stay in a few nights and went down to the basement, which was used as a playroom — the other part was the central heating boiler. I thought this was huge for the size of the house — I reckoned it could have driven a small liner. In the playroom with Sammy and Adam we played cards and listened to their music player, and when Adam left the room for an hour or so, I had to watch myself, for I felt Sammy was coming on a bit, especially when we tried a bit of ballroom dancing. She got a bit close, for I wasn't a good dancer. Still, it was all good fun.

Of course, I had to turn up at the pier to finish my GM course and then I received my draft chit. I was to move to HMS LST 406 now at berth at Bethlehem Fairfield Co., Baltimore, by 6th January 1943. She would have already been commissioned into the Royal Navy on 26th December 1942, so I would miss her commissioning by ten days. Oh dear, that's like missing your first child's christening.

Christmas 1942 was spent on the Chicago pier which had been decorated with flags and bunting. A Christmas dinner of turkey and all the trimmings was laid on, and a large plum pudding and cream, just like we used to have at home before Hitler started his games. Of course, the meal was very large and good, but somehow it was not quite like Mother used to cook. Drink started to flow, but as this was a naval barracks, it was all in moderation, not as expected for an American Christmas party.

Later, when the top brass departed to their own hideaway clubs, the men started to really let their hair down. Girlfriends started to arrive and the music seemed to get louder, and of course the jitterbugs started to jitter. In fact, three of the naval band joined in with their instruments. The whole atmosphere seemed to change, everyone was more friendly and the drinks really began to flow. I never did find out what time I got my head down. I know I didn't return to my digs that night, although I did ring Carl and Greg to let them know I wouldn't be back that night. I do remember I went into the city a day or two before Christmas and brought small presents for each of the family: boxes of chocs and smellies for the girls , and cigs and a tie for the boys (I think).

By the time 6th January arrived I had said my goodbyes to the family and thanked them for their kindness once again. I sometimes wonder if they are still about. I remember once I went home on leave and Mother mentioned that an American girl in USA army uniform had called at the door asking of me — Mother didn't make anything of this, so I heard no more as she could not remember the girl's name.

LST 406

The time had come for my departure from Chicago to my next home, HMS LST 406, now waiting for me in the docks of Baltimore. Once again, I was on my way, kit bag topped up and bulging, hammock rolled up and tidy, suitcase lid straining on the hinges — perhaps soon I would have a place of my own to stow away all my possessions. I found out that I was the only one of my class going to Baltimore. I was issued with a ticket for an overnight coach which was to move off on the 4th January at 7 o'clock in the evening. The coach would travel non-stop, except for comfort stops, and coffee and cookies could be obtained on board. A spare driver was carried to comply with the law, for I think the distance to Baltimore was about 1,000 miles and the journey usually took about 18 hours. Sometimes they would change coaches on long-distance runs; I expect it depended on the condition of the coach. I don't think the distance we were about to embark on was considered long in America.

It turned out to be a good but boring journey, for we were travelling throughout the night and slept most of the time. In fact, I don't remember much of the countryside, and we arrived in the city early in the afternoon. I was dropped off in the city centre — complete with kit bag, hammock and suitcase and I was dead-tired. First thing was to find a watering hole for a strong mug of coffee and then a taxi to the new 406 — excitement mounting!

The taxi stopped at the police office, where I was allowed into the dockyard and shown to where my ship was berthed. I alighted and stood with my belongings around me just staring at the enormous ship that spread out in front of me. It seemed huge to me for I expected something like the small pleasure steamers that usually ply between beaches during the summer holidays. In fact, the LST was a real full-size landing ship, so I think now would be the time to try to explain what this modern large "barn of a ship" looked like and why they were built in their hundreds in the 1940s.

The LST was designed as an all-welded hull, their primary function being to transport tanks, vehicles and troops to be disembarked directly onto beaches. A port or harbour with cranes was simply not required. The LST was built to a length of almost 328 feet, with a beam of about 50 feet, and height of the top deck would be about 35 feet. They had to be shallow enough to run up onto beaches and stable enough to cross the seas, which was overcome by a system of ballast tanks. A large anchor with winch was provided at the rear, and known as a Kedge anchor. At a carefully predetermined spot on the run up to the beach, the Kedge anchor was let go. This was then used to haul the vessel off the beach when it was ready to depart.

The bow doors opened to reveal a watertight ramp which was lowered to give access to the tank deck, which was 230 feet long and 30 feet wide and 11 feet high. An elevator was provided to raise vehicles up to the upper open deck. Accommodation for the troops was on both sides of the main deck and comprised seating, messing, lavatory and shower facilities, and bunks. Armaments comprised of one 12-pounder, situated aft, and six Oerlikon guns — four mounted around the wheelhouse area, and two fitted on the forward area of the upper deck.

The LSTs were used in a variety of roles. Ammunition sometimes filled the tank space, as did mobile artillery, motor transport and food rations. POWs were transported in the tank space, and sometimes the tank space was converted for floating ambulances. The whole warship was manned by about one hundred men and officers. The officers would include Lieutenant Commander as CO, two Lieuten-ants, a Sub-Lieutenant and an Engineer Officer. The lower deck was petty officers, signalmen, telegraphists, electricians, cooks, stewards, sick-berth attendants and supplies assistant (Jack Dusty), seamen, and of course, me. All this and sometimes much more.

The GM V12 power was supplied by two 1,800 HP twin-shaft 2-stroke GM V12 diesel engines giving a maximum speed of just over 10 knots. So there you have it, a metal box almost like a small town, everyone on board with a skill or trade to keep the whole town going, and hopefully to help beat the Nazis who had almost taken over our world.

These sorts of thoughts went through my head as I stood there looking up at the strange ugly ship that was to be my home for the next couple of years or so, if our luck stayed.

At the top of a steep gangplank stood a lone sailor on guard duty and he called me up. He had a pad and ticked off my name, and then pointed me in the direction of the Officer of the Watch. Everywhere was fresh paint and there was a smell of newness in the air; even the Officer of the Watch looked new, and I certainly felt new. The Officer of the Watch seemed a normal sort of chap and we talked for a while. He told me he had only been on board a couple of weeks and he said the skipper was quite a good sort, whose name was Lt. Commander H J Chaloner, RNR and no doubt I would be meeting him in the near future. In the meantime I had to meet Chief Petty Officer Frank Austin, ERN who was to be my immediate superior.

Frank came up to me with a greasy piece of cotton waste in one hand with his other oily hand held out to shake, "Ere, nice to meet you, mate. I'm Frank, sometimes known as Bunny." "I'm Gord, sometimes known as Shorty," I replied, "Nice to meet you too." Frank was 5ft 3ins tall, about the same as me. He was a typical Lancastrian who called a spade a spade and loved the sea and ships. The ships had to be propelled by sail or steam though, and in those short few minutes I first met Frank I could tell he hated diesels. "Come on, mate," I said, "These new GM engines are great." He replied, "You wait and see, Gord. These LSTs and those bloody new-fangled engines are right bastards."

Frank was OK and we got on well together. He was a good engineer, but his heart wasn't in it. He loved jazz, he loved steam engines and small tramp steamers that plied the coast around Morecambe Bay, his home town. On the face of it, it looked as though we were going to be good friends, although he was a few years older than me. One of the things we used to enjoy when in ports around the world was to go aboard interesting ships, asking to see the ship's engineer, and then getting shown around all the wonders of steam and also the really large diesel engines, almost the size of a small house — followed of course by a drop of the hard stuff from the friendly engineer.

My next learning curve was to be shown around the ship and then introduced to the basics of how to start and run the machinery under my charge. I was shown my mess and sleeping quarters, where to collect my meals, where to wash, shower, and the toilet facilities. Frank showed me an empty space in the shower room, "That's where a washing machine used to sit — but the RN bastards have had it taken out — there is also a space where an ice-cream machine stood, but that went too. OK for the yanks, but far too good for the likes of us limeys!"

It was only a week or two before I was getting the hang of it all — how to start the two main engines and the three diesel generator engines. During this time I also had to meet our team of stokers. I think there were fourteen, but this number used to alter from time to time. The group were made up of very young lads, and some quite a lot older, a mixture of inexperience and experience. You could tell the older ones — some wore beards and one had even lost his false teeth! Some wore stripes on their arms to show how long they had served. They were all good boys, not a bad one amongst them. There may have been a couple who were on the borderline, but during the three years I served with them, I would not have changed any one of them.

The first time I went down into the main engine room was a bit scary. A watertight door had to be unlocked, whereupon a square pit or hole faced you. You looked down the dark pit with the roar of the two engines bursting out into your ears. Inside the dark hole was an iron ladder attached to the left-hand bulkhead. You then had to step out into the dark hole and work yourself down, rung by rung, passing the door of the engineers' store and then downwards to the engine room. In bad weather this was a nightmare, especially for the first week or so, but it soon became easy and it wasn't long before we almost slid down those iron ladders thinking it was no more than running up and down the stairs at home.

Once down in the engine room it was another world. The noise was terrific, but the atmosphere was cool and clean. The two large engines were white and shiny, as if they were made of ceramic. The lighting was very good and bright, and all the gunge and waste was cleared and out of sight. The bilges were also kept very clean.

There was a desk adjacent to the control tower, where there were two levers for the control of the engine speed, and the telegraph system for the captain to send his command for the control of the engines to the engine room. On the desk was large graph paper which was used every hour to note changes carried out, such as the speed of the engines and the temperatures, etc. I think about twenty checks had to be noted every hour. We even had to go right along the length of the two-drive shaft to check the temperature of the bearings of the shafts, and also the condition of the watertight seals where the shafts went through the stern to the propellers. The engine room could be very busy, especially when moving in or out of ports, and also when beaching; there would be a motor mechanic and one stoker on duty. This was duplicated for the generator engine room.

After four hours of watch-keeping in either room, one would be ready for a spot of shut-eye. The majority of the stokers or motor mechanics had hardly ever experienced watch-keeping for a long period, so we had to learn fast before we had to tackle the North Atlantic with a pack of U-boats let loose.

Within a couple of weeks we were ready to move off, this time back to New York. Everything was ready — fuel, water, oil and food had been taken on board and us eighteen and nineteen-year-olds were brimming over with excitement and hoped that everything and everybody would be in working order.

The "White Duster" was flying in the cold wind as we slowly moved away from the dock mooring. On checking the charts with Frank that night we worked out that we would not be going to sea, because Baltimore was a few miles inland and there was a series of waterways to get through to New York waters. Our amateur chart-reading turned out to be right, for our skipper took us through the inland route which looked for several miles like a canal; in fact, lots of onlookers stood along the canal side and waved us through and cheered the Union Jack flying on our bows.

After several hours we pulled out into the mouth of the Hudson River and then entered New York waterways. That evening we dropped anchor somewhere in the river and then moved off the next morning to our allotted slot in New York harbour. Our first voyage in the 406 had been completed without mishap. We hoped that all our trips would be as quiet as this one.

Early the next morning, we all had to fall in on the upper deck for a talk from the skipper. He thanked us all for how well we had settled down with a new ship and a new crew. He hoped we would be a happy and lucky ship and also a successful one, with all the new and dangerous operations we might be asked to carry out. He then introduced us to his second-in-command. This post was known as "Jimmy the One" in the Royal Navy and sometimes shortened to just "Jimmy" by the lower deck ratings.

We then were dismissed and returned to our own quarters, all of us wanting to go ashore and get a taste of the "Great White Way". Of course, there were lots of things to do in New York — big bands, jazz clubs, Broadway shows, the Stage Door Canteen, and dozens of bars and clubs.

On the first run ashore Frank and I took the subway to Broadway, not for any reason, only that it sounded good and we had to start somewhere. I was still only a "bumpkin" and was "knocked over" by the skyscrapers, the amount of traffic, and the yellow taxis. We visited the Empire State Building — I thought of the film King Kong where the giant gorilla was hanging onto the tower, trying to knock down the aircraft — I bet you younger ones cannot remember that! We then went into a bar for a cold lager, although it was bitter cold outside.

On checking the daily paper, it reported that the British Army in North Africa was doing well and Rommel had been held, and the Eighth Army under General Montgomery was on the offensive (all good news). Then I noticed a very small piece of news: Bing Crosby had been knocked off the top of the Best Crooners chart and a young upstart, Frank Sinatra, had taken his place — who the hell was Frank Sinatra? Later that week I saw Frank Sinatra sing at The Radio City and I have to admit that he was good . . . even for a youngster.

The next few weeks turned into a round of big eats and drinks, visiting musical shows, visiting girlie shows, visiting jazz and jam sessions — great, I know I shouldn't have joined the Navy! There were two shows that really stand out in my mind. One I think was the Benny Goodman Show — he wanted a serviceman from the audience to go on the stage and conduct the band. Who of our lot do you think volunteered?! — Stoker "Raggy Rex", a slim, six-foot, good-looking (AC, DC) 28-year-old sailor. He brought the house down, and the girls went mad. Talk about the Beatles — they had nothing on Raggy. I forget what he won; I believe it was a bottle of Pussers Rum. After that, we had a dinner and night out in a small night club but we all got back to the 406 on time, and all in one piece.

The other show that impressed me and stands out in my mind was at a music hall on Broadway. There was a walkway each side of the auditorium from the upper circle, down to the stage, and on each walkway were stationed about twenty drummers either side, and on the stage was a large orchestra of Guy Lombard's. When the curtain went up they were playing the Bolero, with all the drummers beating and the orchestra belting out the melody. It was great, and the rest of the programme was just as great — not bad for free — tickets from the Stage Door Canteen!

Life at this time was good, but we were getting soft and at times we felt we should be here to help the war effort, not carry on like playboys. Soon we had an awakening — tugs and cranes came alongside and the upper deck was soon stacked with tons of pig iron and the tank's space was filled with boxes of tins of condensed milk and tinned fruit. Even the troops' sleeping quarters were filled with the tins. So it was true, we were now getting ready to return home. It was late March '43 and the buzz going around was that we had to join a convoy at Halifax, Nova Scotia, bound for the UK, we hoped. There were three other LSTs sailing with us, and serving in one of them was a motor mechanic, PO Bert Townsend. I knew Bert because he came from Swindon. I remember he used to drive a hearse, and if ever a funeral passed when I was out walking with Jennie, Bert used to put his thumb up and wink Jennie didn't think that was quite right, but we had to laugh.

The day before sailing, Bert rang me up (we had a phone system between the LSTs) and he said, "Hello, Gord. Do you think you could help me out? We can't start our main engines and as you know we are off with you tomorrow morning." I replied, "I will if I can, try me! What have you been up to?" He replied, "Our fuel lift pump was leaking, so I took it apart and fitted a new gasket behind the front cover — now we cannot bleed the system." Now, it was a bit of luck that I went through that a few days before — the pump front cover had the maker's name pressed on it and when fitting it back on the pump, the name had to be upside down. I know this because I marked the cover before taking it off. I told Bert what to do — take the front cover off and turn it upside down — I didn't tell him how I knew. Lo and behold! Bert rang me back about an hour after. He sounded quite chuffed, and said everything was working OK. He said that before he rang us, he and his engineer officer had rung around several ships and engineering works for help, and they were at their wits' end for they would have been in serious trouble if they missed the convoy. You can guess I was the "bees knees" after that and was promised gulpers when we met again in the UK.

The 406 duly set sail for Halifax and met up with convoy No. SC125 setting sail to Liverpool, hopefully with no problems. It was a large convoy when it came into view and there were several destroyers and corvettes milling around like sheep dogs. We tagged along behind and then, no doubt, received orders where to take up positions. The signal boys were busy with their flashing lights and within an hour we had moved up in the convoy and taken up our correct position. The weather was fair, but cold, and the whole convoy was motoring along at about 8 knots. I had finished my afternoon watch and was now free for four hours, so I spent about two hours on the stern leaning on the deck rails talking to Frank and watching the movements of the different ships and escorts as we made our way back home.

The next morning the weather was good for early March and I was due on watch in the engine room at 12 noon, when I heard a bit of a scuffle on the upper deck. As I was free, I wandered up to the wheelhouse where I saw a couple of seamen escorting Jock Walker, a large Scotsman, down the stairs. He was drunk and could just about stand. He had a glass of whisky in his hand. Jock was a seaman and had been in the RN for about ten years. He seemed like a good bloke when he was sober, but unfortunately he was an alcoholic. Jock, being a "friendly" alcoholic, decided to go up onto the bridge in his bare feet with a glass of whisky to shake the Captain's hand and wish him good luck. In Nelson's day that would have meant 50 lashes, or perhaps walking the plank! As there were no passengers aboard, there were plenty of spare cabins to put him away and lock him up. Every time they went into the cabin with his food, he was drunk with a new bottle of whisky — it was found later that he had bottles hidden away all over the ship. He would be locked away until we arrived in Liverpool, where his warrant or trial would take place.

The rest of the day went well, but we were all rather shaken with this episode and wondering what would happen to Jock. The older hands thought he would get about 90 days' stoppage and dismissed ship — thinking on this and talking with the boys, we thought this might save his life if our first landing went wrong. No sympathy for him then!

After supper I went to the engine room to start the middle watch. Everything was going fine and at about one o'clock the telegraph rang to increase the port engine one thousand revs — this I carried out, but instead of increasing the revs, it decreased the revs. Cripes! I pushed the lever further, but the revs decreased again, and this time the sound of the engine was uneven. The engine then stopped and the starboard engine started to thump and misfire, and then it decided to stop, in sympathy.

During this time, which was only a matter of minutes, the telegraph pointer and bell went mad, as the quartermaster hurriedly pushed the telegraph handle up and down. I lifted the phone to report to the bridge, when all the lights went out. Bloody hell, what's gone wrong? This should sort us out! Soon the engineer officer was shimmering down the ladder, red-faced, just having been woken up by the skipper, because he also had been woken up. We were in complete darkness for only about a couple of minutes, but it seemed hours, when all of a sudden the emergency lights came on. There was a slight cheer, but these were only temporary lights, so we had to get cracking to sort out the trouble quickly.

The first thing was to check the fuel filters, and on taking the first filter off, nothing but water and bits and pieces of rubbish were blocking the filter bowl. That was the first thing to do — remove and change all the fuel filters on both main engines and the three generators, but what about the 24 uni-injectors? They all had to be removed, dismantled and cleared as well. Do I remember what I was taught in Chicago? I eventually discovered that the internal filters, which are made of a substance like pumice stone, had disintegrated and blocked the system in all the 24 uni-injectors. Of course, this would take hours to fix, especially in the semi-darkness of the emergency lighting, so it was reasonable to get the "gennys" going first.

Two stokers and Les, the second motor mechanic, were detailed to change the fuel filters of the generator engines and bleed the system — if this didn't work then they had to report back. The engines did start straightaway. Bingo! Full lights on again. ERA Frank went off with Ginger, a young stoker, to check all of the fuel tanks and report back as soon as possible, then pump out the contaminated tank. Until we got a clean tank, we ran the engines on fuel from two 50-gallon drums which had been filled up by a relay of stokers with buckets. This was arduous work, as they had to descend to the generator room via the iron ladder, carrying buckets of fuel, with the ship rolling badly. With the gennys now running, the main lighting was in uoe and we could all see well enough to repair the 24 uni-injectors to get the 406 moving as soon as possible.

We had been stationary in the Atlantic just drifting and rolling, tossing without any drive, and the convoy had carried on. In wartime all of the convoys and men would be in jeopardy from the U-boat packs that infected the water if the whole convoy stopped. It had taken almost two days to get going and back to normal. We had been without sleep the whole time, but what a relief not to be lolling around the "pond" like sitting ducks. We were now sailing at full speed. No doubt the skipper had contacted headquarters about where to rendezvous with the convoy, and what direction to take to dodge the U-boats. However, it was worked out OK and it wasn't long before we met up with our convoy. So, within three days we were pulling into Liverpool harbour, all safe and sound, but very chastened at the thought of what could have happened if we hadn't sorted out the fuel problem.

The Italian Job

It was late in the evening when we docked alongside in Liverpool. We had all wound down and were pleased to be able to have a good sound sleep — except, of course, the unlucky few who were on duty watch-keeping in the generator room and guarding the ship as usual when in dock. Jock was still locked in a spare cabin; he of course had been let out for exercise, as per the book. Within two days a notice was posted on the board that a warrant would be read on the quarterdeck concerning the seaman, and all the ship's company not on duty would muster on the quarterdeck at 1.00p.m. Thursday. The time duly arrived. We all stood in a circle and the skipper stood on a box and Jock was brought in handcuffed to two Marines. I'm sure Jock was still drunk, for when the warrant was read out, he just said, "All lies. All f***ing lies." He was laughing, nodding and winking to some of his oppos. It was a bit of a farce really. The end of all this was that he was sentenced to thirty days in prison and to be dismissed ship. He was then taken ashore, put in the back of a van and driven away by the two Marines — never to be seen again (by us).

60

Later that day, we were unloaded and the troop space and tank space were cleaned up and made ready to accept troops, vehicles and tanks. We were to proceed to Glasgow and Gairloch Head, with commandos and their equipment, to carry out beaching trials and to prepare for the coming invasion. Everything was now running smoothly, when out of the blue two senior Naval Engineer Officers arrived to make a report on why we broke down with fuel problems. Of course, we were cross-examined, for I don't think they believed that our fuel was as bad as we reported. I did mention that one of the engineers filled a drinking glass from one of the taps in the fuel tank and sipped the fuel remarking in a slightly supercilious drawl, "This seems OK to me." I was disgusted. Did he think we made it up? I nearly asked if he would like a real sippers, or perhaps gulpers?

Early one morning we set off with the commandos to Gairloch Head for more landing trials. I was in the engine room at the time — it was about six o'clock in the morning and we were doing about 10 knots up the Clyde when the signal was given to put the engines in reverse. We then experienced a big judder and thump, and it appeared that we had gone aground. The young navigation officer had steered the ship the wrong side of the channel and we had rammed hard into the sandy sea bed and stuck fast. I slammed the drive lever into reverse and both engine levers to full revs. Despite turning the Clyde into yellow foam from the sand being churned up, the 406 did not budge an inch. We were then instructed to wait.

After about an hour wondering what had happened, we eventually went onto the upper deck. What wonderment! The tide had gone out and we were left perched on our flat bottom about fifty feet from the Clyde in what looked like a green field. There was a crowd of farmers and kids looking up and laughing — talk about Dad's Army! We then had to wait for several hours before two large tugboats came to our rescue. At first the 406 would have none of it, so it was then suggested that all the crew muster on the stern and jump in unison. This we did and eventually helped to shake the ship free. After this embarrassment we were glad to be on our way. We spent about seven or eight weeks in Glasgow stocking up with provisions.

The time had now come to prepare for the real war. Lord Louis Mountbatten visited the LSTs on the Clyde and addressed some of the ships' crews. The powers-that-be were expecting high numbers of casualties, probably in the region of 70% loss of LSTs — this, of course, made us all gulp. During the next few days the LSTs were loaded with trucks, tanks and troops; some of these were from the 12th Canadian Tank Regiment with their tanks.

The LSTs left the Clyde in three convoys over a period of about eight days in late June. En route we called at Gibraltar and Algiers. It was from Algiers that we sailed on 5th July as part of an invasion force bound for Sicily. Other LSTs, ships, landing craft and support ships already out in the Med sailed from Tobruk, Malta and various other ports. Later that day we met up with the full invasion force — the sea was full of ships, of all sorts and sizes. We then took our place in this huge convoy.

Later in the day I was on the upper deck with the engineer officer when we noticed that all of the ships had suddenly turned to the port side except of course the 406. It was only us that had changed course — our steering had broken down! Panic stations once again. It was then back to the instruction manuals to help sort out the steering problems. After what seemed ages we sorted out the emergency steering and we were then able to take up our position in the invasion convoy.

During the night aircraft could be heard and in the twilight parachutists could be seen dropping, unfortunately, into the sea. Loud explosions could be heard — shells exploding amongst the convoy. On entering the large bay at Syracuse we could see that several LSTs were aground on a sandbar about fifty feet from the landing beaches. This caused a huge problem and new landing beaches had to be found by trial and error. We managed to beach the 406, despite being shelled from inland, and several planes came to strafe and drop bombs.

Looking back, the initial landing was not as bad as we had expected. It seemed that the Italians and the Germans had been taken by surprise. Later in the day, while the unloading of the tank space was carried out, several hundred prisoners of war were marched into the loading bay. We had the unenviable task of searching and cross-examining them to make sure they were not carrying any guns or other weapons.

The Italian prisoners appeared to be very frightened. Their kit bags were filled with dirty clothing and stale bread and cheese. One lad that I was searching had a musical instrument, a cornet. I asked him if he played and he said he did. I gave him a tin of 333 cigarettes and he handed the cornet over to me. He seemed quite happy with the situation, but later I felt ashamed to have taken the instrument away from the prisoner. I often think of this situation and wonder if he would have done the same thing if our positions had been reversed.

The weather all day had been fair, the sea was choppy and we were well up on the beach. We were now ready to pull off and return for reinforcements. There were still sporadic air attacks and enemy gunfire, but no reports of casualties to LST crews or ships had filtered through. The Kedge anchor had held fast and we pulled off the beach just as we had practised in Scotland. The 406 was now part of a shuttle service with 30/40 LSTs to carry heavy equipment and men to other beaches and ports as required by the invading armies as they swept far inland. This build-up was to take several months so we got to know most of the North African ports as we loaded up with the British 8th Army and the yanks 1st Army.

It was during this time in Tripoli that I happened to be having a drink in the local with a glass of their own brew and talking to a British soldier when I noticed he had a black cat badge on his sleeve. My brother Dick had been in the Middle East for a few years, and we had not met for at least three years; he also wore that black cat badge, and I happened to have his photograph in my wallet. I showed my companion the photo and he said, "That's our staff sergeant. He's only a couple of miles up the road. I've got a jeep outside; I'll take you to him." We then piled into the jeep and bumbled over a couple of miles of desert. We eventually pulled up behind an army workshop truck and there was Dick in the open back, grinning like a Cheshire cat. Of course, it was talk talk. How I got back to the 406 that night I still cannot remember after 60 years. Later we read an article in the Swindon Advertiser about our meeting. I am glad to say we both survived the war. Dick is now 92 years of age, and I won't tell you my age.

During this time we must have sailed thousands of miles loading up and discharging on the beaches as required. The days at sea were pleasant but we did have our problems when the weather turned against us, as it did in the Med at that time of the year — when it was good, it was very, very, good but when it was bad, it was horrid!

The 406 was turning into a good ship and we were getting proud to be part of her, but in the bad weather she was known as a flat-bottomed bastard! Being flat-bottomed, she would roll and kind of twist and make everyone wonder if she would right herself again. After hitting a large wave the props would lift out of the sea causing the engine to rev up to a screaming pitch and then smash back into the sea causing a huge shudder throughout. This could go on for hours on end so one can imagine what state the Army lads were in after a storm.

Here is the story of how two Swindon brothers — one a soldier and the other a sailor — met in a Mediterranean port, and spent some happy hours together. Staff Sergt Dick Turner of the REME and Gordon Turner who is a motor mechanic in the Navy are the sons of Mr and Mrs J Turner, of 210, County Road Swindon, and it is interesting to note that their father is an old soldier of the last war and was wounded at Ypres.

"Dick" Turner was called up as soon as war was declared and sent to France, where he gained the rank of Staff Sergeant. After Dunkirk he went to Egypt, and served in Greece and Crete. Escaping from Crete he returned to Egypt and subsequently took part in all campaigns which led up to the capture of Tunisia and Sicily.

"Dick" is married, and his wife is living with her parents at 31, Ferndale Road. Before the war he was employed as a motor mechanic at Skurray's.

Gordon, who was also at Skurray's before the war, joined the Navy last July, and in the course of his duties has visited America. He was then attached to landing craft for tanks, and hearing his brother was in the Mediterranean zone, he determined to find him. He searched all the REME camps at the ports he called at, and eventually succeeded in his quest.

This is how the reunion took place, described by brother "Dick" in a letter to his mother. "I was working in the machinery truck and Gordon climbed up in the back. We talked awhile and then Gordon had to be back onboard again, but I saw him again the next day. He slept at our camp and we talked and talked all night long. I was very sorry indeed to say good-bye to him on the jetty, but he has not gone yet, and I may see him again before he sails . . . I hope we both get through this last do OK."

And so say all of us. Good luck, Dick and Gordon!

From Saturday Evening Advertiser,
11 September 1943

In good weather some of them would think it was all great — being able to have a hot shower when you wanted one, playing cards and darts and other games in the mess deck, and clean beds and toilets . . . the life of old Riley! Then it would all happen. The wind would get up, then the rolling and pitching would start and all the different noises, such as banging and howling like banshees, would begin. It wouldn't be long before the toilets started to slop over and some of the crews' lockers would move — in bad storms they would even fall over. After several hours everyone would be at the end of their tether and poor Army boys would be white around the gills and clinging on for dear life to whatever was at hand — and then as suddenly as it started, everything would seem to stop. Peace and quiet would resume.

On taking stock, everything would be chaotic — two or three inches of stinking water slopping through the toilets and mess deck, playing cards, draughts counters and clothes which should have been stowed away, floating about or piled up in a wet heap. What a change would come over the soldiers. All their jealousy of the sailor's life would be gone. "How can you live on a bloody tin can like this? Get us ashore as soon as you can." That's life — the grass is always greener.

Most shuttle trips were not without some incident of note — like the Sunday afternoon when those of us on "make and mend" (Navy term for rest period) would be enjoying the sun and a game of Uckers (Ludo) on the upper deck. I happened to be lazing under the 12-pounder gun platform on the stern with three of my oppos when all of a sudden the gun opened fire (Bang! Crash!). All the pots and pans on the galley shelves fell off, and soot and smoke covered us. Blimey, we thought we had blown up. It turned out that the gun crew had sighted a sub-conning tower about 250 yards ahead — the shell landed right at the base of the conning tower . . . I saw it happen.

The Captain of our Squadron Leader signalled "Good shooting, 406" — but our skipper angrily wanted to know who gave the gun crew orders to open fire! Oh dear! It might have been a friendly sub! I don't think it was though, for our escort destroyer was soon racing through the convoy lobbing out depth charges. Whenever this happened all hell would be let loose. Sirens would blast off, "Action Stations, Action Stations" would be tannoyed over the radio system and the escort destroyers would speed throughout the convoy flying a large black flag.

During Action Stations all the crew would have their own special jobs to do. The engine crews would slide down the vertical ladders to the engine and generator rooms and lock all watertight doors — everyone in the engine rooms was locked in. The tension could almost be cut with a knife. When the escort ship started to lob out depth charges the explosions could be felt through the deck — bearing in mind the LST was flat-bottomed and there was only the engine room bilges and deck plates below to stop our feet getting wet. Action Stations would stay in force until the sub danger had passed, which had to be agreed by the Destroyers' top brass. When giving the stand down the whole convoy would be advised and the Destroyers would race off, guarding the convoy, and life aboard would return to normal.

The war in Italy was now progressing well, although to us it seemed that the initial push had slowed down. Further landings had taken place, both the British and American Armies had crossed the Straits of Messina into Italy and the 406 was still running in supplies of ammunition to different beaches along the coast. By this time several LSTs had been lost or badly damaged by shore fire. LST417 was hit by a torpedo bomb. We were never told exactly what was happening to other ships, but by word of mouth it would get around if anything disastrous had happened. We did hear that six of 417 crew had been killed on our sister ship.

That day we made it into Tripoli. The harbour was full of landing ships and assault craft so we guessed another landing was being planned — no doubt to cut off Naples and also Monte Casino as both of these objectives were proving to be a thorn in our side. The next two days consisted of carrying out service work to the engines, etc. etc! So we all felt we needed a day off. Fred Rostrum and Cliff Hensby, my oppos in the engine room, and I decided to walk into Tripoli, about five miles from the docks. It was a beautiful morning.

As soon as we reached the dock gates I could hear a band playing Georgia on my Mind. I stopped and said, "Listen, I bet that's Nat Gonella playing that trumpet." Nat was a well-known jazz trumpeter and my idol from when I played a trumpet in a dance band in the days before I had even heard of the Royal Navy. By now that seemed a lifetime ago. My mates were not impressed and we continued our walk, talking about everything under the sun, but mostly about home. The music carried on and got louder as we reached the city outskirts. I was right — there on an old-fashioned bandstand was the Royal Tank Regiment Band and Nat Gonella was leading them. Just think, there was I, watching and listening to my idol. I couldn't afford to see him at home — we had no TV in those days — and now I had travelled thousands of miles through storms at sea and one or two bombs to see my idol Nat. Talk about luck! We shook hands and had a few words but I forgot to get his autograph — can't think of everything.

We eventually walked into the city and had a well-earned drink of "hooch" out of cut-off jam jars. There were no ordinary drinking glasses left in North Africa in those days — our drinking glasses had most often started life as jam jars or bottles. They were filled with oil to the correct size and a red hot poker plunged into the oil. The glass would then split smoothly to the oil line leaving a very usable vessel. We had a good day, a good meal (no doubt goat or camel) and then a look around the shops and bazaars for "Rabbits" (Royal Navy language for gifts) to take home to our girlfriends and Mums and Dads. Imagine arriving back in Dover and going through the Customs with your hammock and kitbag on your shoulder and a gruff voice shouting, "Where do you think you are going, sailor? What have you got in that bag?" and you reply, hurrying on, "Oh, only a few rabbits.' That would probably cost a couple of days" jankers!

We spent a week or so tied up alongside in Tripoli harbour and that, of course, meant we could spend some time ashore and help make up for the very dry days aboard. We had one scare: the second day alongside, there was a huge explosion from the dock area and a vast column of black smoke could be seen. Of course, everyone was put on stand-by. It turned out to be one of the LCT landing craft being loaded with ammunition when it blew up, causing severe damage to that part of the docks. We were lucky to be about a quarter of a mile from the incident so we were not really involved. Just one of those near happenings!

By now we were seaworthy again and we moved the 406 to a loading bay where the 51st Highland Division was waiting to start loading. They looked a formidable fighting force — brown as berries, with their weapons, hand grenades, pots and pans and belts of ammo hanging round their bodies. We heard that they had been in North Africa before the war started, and no doubt had forgotten what it was all about. They had been part of the 8th Army and fought from Tobruk and

Alamein. They soon made themselves at home on the 406 and enjoyed the comfort of a real hot shower and bunk beds. They loaded the tank space with large trucks coupled to huge artillery guns; it could be seen that they knew their business and we felt proud that they were on our side. When we were in England we used to read about the North Africa campaigns in the morning papers — and now we were amongst and part of that war.

Time seemed to drag now waiting for the next phase, so some of us spent the time catching up writing letters home to our loved ones. Writing letters home was one of the most important times of the day for a lot of us. I know that most of the married blokes found life very difficult and when off duty would mope around and seldom go ashore with the rest of us or their mates.

It was, of course, very difficult writing home. We had to watch we did not write about the "war operations" or where we had been or where we were going. What was left of interest to a teenage girl? Perhaps "smoochy" love — or what we would do when we got home.

Then we would suddenly remember — every one of our letters would be read and censored by one of our officers.

I don't know how I managed it, but I know I wrote almost every day and Jennie also wrote back every day. Often the letters would arrive very late and when they did arrive it would be in bundles of six or seven. Sometimes when I wrote a "special" letter I would think of an officer looking at me as if he was censoring it — especially if I was writing something derogatory about one of his kind! We would of course put in things we wanted them to know, such as how bad the food was. Somehow, I think I got a lot of comfort from writing letters home to Jennie. We were such a long time apart, and didn't know how or when it would all end — it seemed years ahead before we could even think of going home. We appeared to have got to know ourselves, and each other, better by putting our thoughts to paper.

We had now been alongside docks in Tripoli for several days, already loaded with the Scots Guards and the equipment, when we were informed that we would be sailing the next morning. On 6th September '43 the invasion convoy of 20 LSTs sailed from Tripoli. Later that day we were informed by the skipper on the journey that this new operation was called "Avalanche". The objective was to land the Allies at Salerno, so they could move round the coast and capture the vital port of Naples.

During the voyage the Army boys received lectures from their officers, with maps spread out on the upper deck under the blue Mediterranean sky. The ship's radio was tuned to the British Forces when the momentous announcement was heard, "Italy has capitulated." We couldn't believe it. Did this mean the end was in sight? The newsreader followed with a wonderful piece of oratory:

Mussolini's dreams lay in ashes — proud pretender brought to his knees — a dynasty had passed into oblivion; then "click" from the tannoy, " 'ands to supper! 'ands to supper"! Empires may crumble and history might be in the process of being rewritten, but at half past six in the Royal Navy, 'ands still had to go to supper. Perhaps it's that adherence to tradition that makes the Royal Navy great.

As quoted from the LST book,
Ships Without Names.

Night had now fallen. It was calm, visibility was good and we were now creeping along the coast with the engines turning over slowly and quietly. The bombardment then opened up. It was deafening and the flashes were continuous and blinding. We had thought that the capitulation of the Italians would have made things easier, but how wrong we were.

As we slowly moved into the Gulf of Salerno we passed quite close to a Royal Navy monitor (large gunboat with four battleship guns) side-on to the beach. She blasted off her great guns and recoiled just as we slid by. The noise was terrific and the recoil movement of the great ship felt on the 406 was as if we had been hit with a huge wave. The force had knocked our lighting generators off the board and we were left in darkness. It was panic stations for a few moments until our generator room boys put things to rights.

In the dawn light we could see we were now in a huge bay with dozens of large and small ships and an assortment of landing craft and LSTs standing off the beaches, waiting for the word to "go" from their command to race for the beaches to off load the Army and their heavy equipment. The really brave boys had already charged the beaches to make way for the landing ships and set the ball rolling for a full-scale invasion.

Then horror! It was noticed that the sea had started to erupt all around. The enemy was fighting back and shells were falling everywhere. The Germans were firing their 88mm guns into the invasion fleet. During the day, several LSTs received damage — wounding and killing some of the crews from the shelling and bombing. Our 406 was very lucky and did not receive any damage.

The landing was a success and we made our way back to Tripoli to load up for another run to Salerno. We did, however, hear some bad news during our next landing. We made enquiries regarding how the Scots fared after they left the 406 for the first assault and it seemed that about 30% were killed or wounded during an air raid the first night. This news caused much sadness to all of the crew, for a great comradeship existed between us. During our stay in Tripoli we had been out for a drink with them and also played Tombola and cards and swapped yarns. It's good to make new friends, even for a little while — especially people like us who are on board with the same people for months on end.

We made many sailings to Salerno from various ports, packing up equipment and stores as required. Each time we had to pass Monte Casino and always had a grandstand view of the terrible fight with the

British and Polish Army at the bottom of the Mount and the Germans entrenched in the monastery above. At night the shells and rockets could be seen, like a firework display, but much more frightening and deadly.

Whilst at Salerno waiting for troops to unload, things had become quiet. We used to wander over to some of the other LSTs and swap news. There were also rumours going around about new weapons that the Germans were using. One I remember was about a remote-controlled tank that was being put in the sea and would then crawl up the beach to smash shells into the landing fleet. Oh yes, we had heard it all before. Perhaps it could be true!

One morning when we were waiting to unload, Les, Cliff and myself decided to look at an LST that had been badly damaged and abandoned. They had already unloaded and pulled off the beach when they were bombed, and a bomb had exploded in the engine room. As the damage was serious, they decided to go for the nearest beach. When they opened the bow doors and lowered the ramp, Germans rushed up the ramp firing from their hips with Tommy guns. The beach was still in enemy hands! The LST crew fought them off and sought refuge in a cave. They were eventually rescued by a Royal Navy landing party from one of the warships in the bay. Stories like this abounded, perhaps put around by the enemy, but we just had to close our ears to these tales for, after all, we were now on the winning side, or so we believed.

The best bit of news was just a few days after Naples had fallen. We could now dock in Naples and would not have to plough backwards and forwards to Tripoli hoping to miss the Jerry bombers, subs, and E-boats. We entered Naples docks about a week later and it looked like a fallen city — not a great deal of damage, but everything looked poor. The people, especially the women, had not eaten for days and the children were hungry and begging for sweets, chocolates and anything at all to eat. It seemed to us that the Germans had taken all the food when they left. There were beggars everywhere — young men, old men, women and children. The women, I think, suffered the most. Most of the men were still in the Army, or at least wearing the uniform.

In Naples we loaded up in the inner dock, which appeared to be at the end of a back street; there was just about room for two LSTs. As soon as we stopped moving, about fifty children crowded around the bow doors, all holding out their hands for food. They still do that now in Africa, sixty years after the war, but in 1944 this was all new to us and it was difficult to know how to handle it. Anyway, "Jack Tar" found a way and soon set to and set up tasty snacks of bread and cheese, etc. etc. and plenty of sweets from Jack Dusty's store to satisfy most of the kids.

When things had settled down and we got used to them, we invited a couple of the lads, about 11 years old, aboard to try their hand at cleaning. They loved it, especially when we paid them with "eats". One of the boys did stay on board for a "ride" up to Salerno. This had to be kept very hush-hush, for we could have been "hung, drawn, and quartered" if anything had happened to him. We didn't worry so much about it, for we were young and it seemed a good idea at the time.

One of the incidents that nearly caused a riot was when several bumboats swarmed around two of the docked LSTs, including the 406. A bumboat was a small rowing boat with two people selling fruit or jewellery. They would shout up to the deck and anyone buying would throw down a rope and eventually pull up their purchase after a price was agreed — in this case it would be a tin of corned beef or a packet of fags. Of course this was considered to be "not on" in wartime, at least to the yankee dock police who patrolled the dock in small, speedy gunboats. This time the bumboat was manned by an old man and a girl of about 25 — however, it was not fruit they were selling, but it was for a look at the beautiful girl's "wot's it". This, of course, caused mayhem. Most of the crew of the LSTs were crowding the upper deck to gain a grandstand view, shouting remarks, etc. and offering all sorts of payment. The Chief Petty Officer blew his whistle and demanded the deck to be cleared, but then someone threw a small tin of corned beef which struck the Chief on his head knocking off his peaked cap. This had to be the end or we would all be sent home in disgrace — but no, it all started to escalate.

The yankee police boat came speeding to the LSTs, the policeman waving his arms and shouting to the bumboat to move. Of course, this got the backs up of us Brits on the LST who told the yank to "clear off" in good old-fashioned language. As the bumboat did not move off, the yank started to fire at the bottom of their wooden rowing boat with his Tommy gun. The old man and his daughter were panicking and almost turned their boat over. In the meantime, "sailors being sailors", we set up a couple of hosepipes, aiming the hoses at the yank, knocking him head-over-heels into the sea. When this happened, all of the excited crew cheered before disappearing below decks and into their own little hideaways.

We all worried what would happen the next day — but nothing was said, no doubt because we were set to sail to Taranto, the great Italian naval base, to load up with equipment required at Salerno. No more was heard of this fracas except it made us wonder what sort of world this was when an old man had to take his daughter out to expose herself so they could eat that day, and what about us who nearly fought each other just to get a glimpse?

The next morning we set off to sail for Taranto on the east coast, a journey of about three days. We arrived late afternoon and tied up outside the harbour. There were several LSTs and other ships all in line waiting to go into the inner harbour. Later in the day we were all ordered to go out to sea and then return the next morning when we received instructions for our turn. We went to sea baffled and wondering why. It was later explained that every day the dive-bombers would come out of the sun at the same time to dive-bomb the ships outside the harbour. Owing to the damage to the ships and the shipwrecks sunk in the harbour, there was very little ground cover or time left to chase the planes off. The Allies' plan was to move out all the waiting ships and replace them with two Ack-Ack cruisers — large warships filled with anti-aircraft guns, pompoms and rocket launchers, etc. On our return to the harbour the next day we were told that the outcome of this disruption was great — every one of the dive-bombers had been shot down. This news did wonders for morale.

After docking in Taranto we obtained permission to look around the harbour where half the Italian ships were lying in wrecked and burnt-out condition. We took our run-about motorboat and four of us, Fred, Cliff, Les and myself, motored past cruisers, destroyers and submarines, all damaged and, to our eyes, beyond repair. New warships were being built and were still in the stocks. The Allied bombing must have been terrific and no doubt one of the causes of the Italian capitulation.

On our sail back to the 406 we noticed a sunken merchant ship of about 10,000 tons. The top deck and bridge was still out of water so we decided to climb aboard. The cabins and crew's quarters were still intact, but there were letters and personal bits and pieces all over. We also found a crate of medals for victory in the desert and Italy so this ship, we could now see, was German. Looking out of the wheelhouse onto the fo'c'sle, we saw the body of a man floating in a foot of water filling the deck well. He was dressed in pants and singlet, his arms outstretched, and his fingers had most of the flesh eaten away (no doubt by fish). His body

80

was bloated and the singlet was stretched like a drum skin. I still remember this because someone said his body looked like a drum and then picked up a spent bullet case and tossed it onto the body — there was only a splash, not a boom like we all expected. After this we all decided to get back to the 406 and return to "normal".

At eleven o'clock "Up spirits" was tannoyed and the off-watch crew queued up for their tot of rum. The mess men collected the Petty Officers' neat rum, eight tots of rum for our mess. We were "neaters", that is, we were allowed neat rum, as opposed to the 2-in-1 for ordinary seamen whose rum was diluted by two parts water. As ours was neat, we used to put one tot into a separate bottle for later use, topping up the daily ration with water and shaking it up. It was still virtually neat, and we had the bonus of extra rum for later use, which of course was strictly against the rules if discovered. A tot was an eighth of a pint, and so after eight days we had collected one pint of rum for special occasions.

Of course, this extra spirit could also be used for all sorts of bribes and payments, etc. If you wanted something special done, such as washing or ironing of shirts, for instance, you could pay with rum. It might be "sippers" for a small job or "gulpers" for a larger favour. When paying for favours you handed your glass of rum over and the recipient would take a sip . . . and you would watch very hard to ensure that he took only a sip. For "gulpers" you would have to watch even harder with your hand raised ready to snatch the glass away. It was quite an education trying to barter with rum!

On Christmas Day after "Up spirits" all chiefs and Petty Officers were invited to the wardroom for a drink with the skipper, listening to his talk about the previous year and what to expect in the future. That Christmas we learned that nothing startling was to come but that another landing was expected soon. After the skipper's whisky we all moved around the wardroom for a chat with the officers of different divisions. What with the skipper's whisky and "sippers" from old friends, we were all getting very merry by the time we moved to our own mess. It was a good job we didn't have to drive home — only a few yards to walk down the gangway to our mess, and no breathalysers waiting.

The mess had been decorated with Christmas cards and anything we could get our hands on. The mess man had made a great job of laying the table for eight. Somehow he had obtained silver ashtrays and silver containers for holding cigarettes from the wardroom. Before dinner could be served we had to entertain several Chiefs and Petty Officers from other LSTs, visiting to drink our good health and of course vice versa . . . with the illicit rum we'd saved! It wasn't long before we were all "pie-eyed" but we managed to demolish the wonderful Christmas fare after our visitors had left. It was then into our bunks to crash our heads (sleep) for the next four or five hours. A good time was had by all!

The following morning we all felt fragile, back to work and another run to Salerno. Following this we had to take an LCI (small landing boat) to a town past Salerno. For some reason it had to be towed and the weather was deteriorating very badly. It was well into the afternoon before we could collect the LCI and by the time we were on our way it was getting very dark. By now the weather was even worse and it was decided that some poor matelot had to stay on the quarterdeck to keep an eye on our towed LCI.

The night was terrible — the old 406 was standing on her head and rolling like a good 'un. When morning and light eventually came the poor matelot was looking very sick and was trying to explain where our towed LCI had gone. The tow rope, which was about two inches thick, had broken and the boat had disappeared into the angry sea.

We never did find out who wanted the boat or if it was part of a secret mission. I think we must have sent a message to HQ that we had lost their boat and it may have been to Winston! We eventually returned to Naples and never heard any more about the lost boat.

The following three weeks was taken up loading arms, food and troops for the front line around Salerno, but it now appeared that another landing was imminent when we arrived back in Naples. More and more LSTs and ships of war were arriving, and the harbour road was filling up with troops — British and American, and their equipment.

It was now 23rd January and early in the morning we were loaded to the gunnels with troops and equipment and set sail to meet up with another invasion convoy. We were told this time it was a small town, Anzio. This name was to become famous for the fierce fighting that took place there. The harbour and bay was constantly bombarded from the German shore batteries and aircraft. Anzio harbour was very small, a typical seaside resort, sandy beaches and a very shallow harbour, less than 8-10 foot draught and it could only accept two LSTs.

The town had received severe damage, mostly by enemy shelling and bombing. Landing on the beach was difficult owing to the rocky conditions of the beaches either side of the harbour. To unload the Army trucks we had to use a pontoon. Several had been brought out, fixed to the side of LSTs with pontoon side fixing. This was the first beach we were unable to run straight onto, so the pontoons were there for the LSTs to use.

It turned out to be very difficult; the pontoons had to be anchored very firmly as the heavy LSTs had to run straight up to the pontoons with their doors open and ramps down. The ships only had to nudge against the end and the pontoon would swing and rock, easily knocking the trucks off the pontoon and into the sea. Of course, we overcame this problem, but it did increase the time it took to unload.

The first time we tried nudging up, there was a beach marshal standing on the pontoon with a megaphone, shouting out his orders. He was a Lt Commander so we had to keep a straight face and not laugh when our nudge was slightly harder. The pontoon bucked and he was tipped over into the sea. Of course, he ranted and raved but we soon fished him out of the cold 'oggin — just one of the things that happens in war!

LSTs were now sailing back and forth between Anzio and Naples, which continued for about two months, almost always under shellfire or bombing attacks. One of our biggest problems at Anzio was a 280mm gun mounted on railway wheels concealed in caves and hills. As far as can be ascertained, "Anzio Annie" never actually hit any LST, but the boom and the whoosh of her shells would strike fear into LST crews every time they came back to Anzio.

On our return to Naples it was noticed that Mount Vesuvius looked different; there was a ring of fire around the top and smoke and fumes were spewing out. There was also a nasty smell of sulphur all around. When we went out onto the upper deck the next morning it looked as if there had been a snowfall — it was of course white ash and small grains of lava. This went on for several days, by which time the lava "grains" were about the size of peas and the smell of sulphur was overpowering. Walking the pavements or decks was like walking on about two inches of gravel.

The next week or so the eruption of Vesuvius became worse and the lava flow was now running in little rivulets down the sides of the mountain — several houses in the small villages were destroyed and lava the size of rocks was falling out of the sky. Luckily, Naples harbour was far enough away for us to miss the real trouble. We did hear that the Army boys did a great job saving some of the small villages by using bulldozers and troops to dig deep trenches to allow the lava to run past the outskirts.

Once the mountain and the internal fire and power had settled down, the gravel-like lava started to disappear from the roads and the sulphur smell started to get weaker. So it seemed the worst was over; this eruption was not going to be another disaster like Pompeii. At least the British and American Armies were on hand with their equipment to help save lives and homes.

News coming back from the front was quite good, and also we were told that LSTs were in short supply at home. This sort of news was called "buzzes" by RN crews. Most buzzes had some truth in them, so it now appeared that our work in the Med was coming to an end. With a bit of luck we could be back in the UK within a month or so. We were still going to Anzio and back the next day and it was reported that Rome would fall in the next week or so.

We, of course, were going ashore for a few drinks most evenings, and it was noticeable that Italy was coming back to life again. A large building near the docks had been opened up as a service club, drinking den, or British pub — call it what you will. I forget what it was named but we all enjoyed it — the bar was good and cheap and there were plenty of tables and chairs. The beer was sold in large one-litre tin cans. The whole top of the cans would be removed, and one drank out of it so there was no washing up of glasses.

After about two hours' drinking, the table would have about a dozen or two large empty cans taking up room, so what was one to do? Pile up the empty cans like skittles in a pyramid in the centre of the table. Just imagine about twenty-five tables, each with about two or three pyramids of cans standing about two feet high. What would happen then? Some idiot would think one of the pyramids was too high, take aim, throwing a spare can, knocking over the offending pyramid — Crash! Bang! Crash! Everyone would then start aiming and it wouldn't be long before the space above the tables would be alive with flying cans ... more dangerous than Anzio.

We had some great evenings in this new club, and very little real trouble. Most of the lads staggered back "home" singing old RN songs, best now forgotten. Our "home" of course was Number 406. Sometimes it was more difficult to get back on the 406 after a great night out, and that was when we were anchored in a bay. We would go ashore in the "liberty boat", which was laid on by one of the ships — it could be our ship's boat on one of the other RN ships in the harbour.

We would of course take it in turns whose boat to use and also who was going to drive it. I used to enjoy driving the liberty boat, and it was quite an education listening to the "liberty men" made up of lower deck ratings and officers of all ranks, most of them "three parts to the wind". To get back on board, the liberty men would have to wait at a spot in the docks at an agreed time (like waiting for a bus back home). All would be fine until we started to find our ship — something which was almost impossible in the dark. The ships anchored in the bay would have moved by the current on tide, and instead of the bow facing, say, a building on the beach, it would now be facing out to sea.

Of course, there was always a "blackout" in force so it was very difficult to pick out a name or ship's number among the dozens at anchor in the harbour. We would have to pick out the ship we thought might be ours and then shout, hoping those on watch about thirty feet away on the upper deck would hear us and perhaps know where the ship we were looking for was anchored. Bearing in mind, as mentioned before, all the ships would have been moved by the sea currents, it was by no means an easy feat. When eventually finding our ship, someone would throw down a rope ladder which would usually land about three feet above our boat, or else would crash down on the heads of the liberty men waiting to be taken off below, giving them a good excuse to complain of a headache in the morning.

Now, to climb aboard via a rope ladder was a very hazardous experience, what with having two or three bottles tucked in your shirt and two or three pints of beer inside your belly, and having to leap onto the hanging ladder with the liberty boat bobbing up and down. At the top you would be grabbed by two burly crew members and dragged aboard to safety, hoping the Officer of the Watch had not noticed that you were smuggling aboard three bottles of booze and some rabbits in your pocket which you had forgotten about. We usually got away with it and turned into our bunks feeling happy — until our feet started to rise and we started to curse the rolling of the old 406. Then we would realise that we were at anchor in a calm bay — blimey! They must have some strong beer out there!

We continued the shuttle service to Anzio and to several new beaches further up the coast towards Rome, which was still in German hands. Bad weather continued well into February and some of the LSTs had started to return to the UK. Of course, we were wondering when our time would come, as the shuttle service to Anzio was now winding down. Enemy activity was very light, only a couple of air raids, which soon broke up after a few Ack-Ack rounds fired by the escort ships.

There was a U-boat alarm which turned out to be a Free French submarine, so we started to believe the Jerries must be getting short of equipment and supplies. Of course they had nothing like our LSTs to help keep their Army going (like us!).

By the middle of March we could feel the Italian operation was drawing to a close. Rome had fallen and we had received orders to make for Casablanca. The journey would take a week or so and with luck there should be no trouble from the Jerries. We sailed from Naples in a convoy of seven LSTs and escorts. On the second morning the weather was perfect, the sky was bright blue and we all felt at peace with the world (at least I did), when all of a sudden an unholy noise erupted that blasted us out of our peaceful reverie. Hee-Haw! Hee-Haw! The lead LST had tethered a donkey on the upper deck and he was loving it. He started to bray for about two hours in between rolling and kicking on bales of straw which had been laid out

89

lovingly by an "official donkey crew". The skipper had purchased the donkey for his kids when he got home — talk about "rabbits"! We got used to hearing a donkey braying in the middle of the Med — very much better than the sound of "Action Stations! Action Stations!" blasting out of the ship's tannoy.

The journey to Casablanca continued as planned. We passed Gib on our right and turned left into the Atlantic . . . we must have used AA road maps! We were now back into the war zone amongst the U-boat packs.

Casablanca was a very busy port crowded with LSTs, troops and their equipment of tanks and motor vehicles, all waiting to be transported back to the UK. We docked alongside, for we had to wait for docking ramps so that the tanks and vehicles could be driven through the opened bow doors. When going ashore we had to use a gangplank until the ramps were ready, but to return to the ship we had to use a ladder because there was a very high tide and the ship had dropped several feet. We had forgotten that the Atlantic had a tide, but the Med did not — something to bear in mind when we beached in France.

During the next week there were 22 LSTs waiting and loading up for their return to the UK. There were 2,700 Free French troops, 235 British troops, 346 yanks, 701 vehicles and seven bags of mail (no doubt most of the letters were for me!). Whilst all that was going on for a few weeks we managed several runs ashore for whatever a matelot goes ashore for, and also to stock up with a few more rabbits — couldn't afford a donkey though!

From Casablanca on 11th April 1944, 22 LSTs set sail to embark the above troops and vehicles at Swansea and Port Talbot. The 406 docked at Port Talbot early in May with all the convoy intact. There is very little to report about the journey. The weather at times was very bad, although we did have several warm and sunny days, but we were all so "over the moon" at arriving back in the UK safe and sound that the weather failed to register.

The Build-up to D-Day

Our arrival at Port Talbot caused quite a stir amongst the locals, and crowds came along to see the landing ships and talk to the crews. All the troops, tanks and vehicles were unloaded within a few days; even the donkey went ashore and was soon grazing in a nearby field. He was in his element jumping and kicking and racing around the field, and of course "hee-hawing" to his heart's content.

It wasn't long before the locals put on a meal and drinks, etc. for the crews. It turned out to be quite a party — speeches, back-slapping and, of course, singing . . . I think it was held in the local church hall.

The stay in Port Talbot was very short and within three days we were on our way to Harwich. When we arrived we were greeted with the news that we were in for intensive training — how to drop the rear Kedge anchor and how to open the bow door when breaching, etc. Our senior officer blew his top and asked if carrying out full-scale real invasions for twelve months was not good enough training. It turned out that the Harwich authorities had us down as fresh from the US boatyard!

However, the main thought on our minds was, of course, home leave! Leave for everyone was soon worked out — only a skeleton crew was to be left aboard; the rest of us went home for two weeks. Rail warrants were soon organised and kit bags packed with clothes (blue, now we were back in the UK), and of course our prized "rabbits". I don't remember the journey home — train from Harwich to London and then onwards from Paddington to Swindon. We didn't have personal mobiles in those days, and our Mums and Dads did not have a phone at home, so we just had to get home as soon as possible and turn up on the doorstep, hoping everything was OK.

It was mid-April, very sunny but cold . . . perhaps that was because we had just arrived back from the Med. The train arrived at Swindon station during the afternoon and I still had to get home with a heavy kit bag and a large suitcase. There were one or two old cars waiting outside with a notice saying "Taxi" on the rear panel — of course they were not "real" taxis like those in London. I decided to "think big" and hire one. Home was only about a mile down the road, so it wasn't long before we pulled up outside No 210 County Road. The taxi driver was a young lady, so things had changed a bit since I'd been away.

I hammered hard on the front door because Mum was very deaf and it wasn't long before Dad opened the door. His eyes lit up and he beamed. "Hello, son. We wondered what time you would arrive." Then Mother came to the door, announcing, "I've just put the kettle on to make a cuppa." We then all went into the kitchen and started to talk, bombarding each other with questions. "How have you been? When are you going back? Where's Jen? Have you heard from Dick?"

Tea soon arrived boosted with a huge slice of seed cake, homemade of course. Mother was always a good cook and no doubt we were in for a good Sunday dinner of roast beef, Yorkshire pudding, and all the trimmings, from coupons saved over many months for just such an occasion. On the whole the meals were not bad on board ship, but nothing could touch Mother's home cooking.

It wasn't long before Jennie came in from work on her bike and also brother Brian who came in from school. Brian was 13 and he had shot up to about 5ft 6ins, leaving me behind. The time had now come to hand round the "rabbits", but that would have to wait until I unpacked my case and kit bag.

By now I was getting anxious about Jennie. I had been home for at least three hours and hadn't had even one kiss or cuddle. Would have to get around to it soon! I eventually opened up my kit bag and produced the magic "rabbits". They all seemed to be pleased with the wartime presents I had bought: underwear and stockings for the ladies, and silk scarves, brass trinkets, cuff links, etc. for the men, and "smellies" for both sexes — lots of "oohs and aahs" from all concerned.

When sanity returned, Jennie and I decided it was time to make for Jennie's home to see her Mum and Dad. We would have to catch the bus. The likes of us did not own motorcars in those days and taxis were for

use on special occasions only and I had already used a
taxi to get home from the station.

Bill and Flo were both pleased to see me again (I
believed them!), and they were both fit and well. They
were good sports and Bill was always full of fun; in fact
at times he often embarrassed me with some of his
jokes. Flo didn't seem to mind, but at times she might
venture to say, "Oh, Bill, stop it!" I remember one day
they were having a party in the front room when he put
a plastic dog's poo — a wicked-looking one — on the
front room carpet. He said, angrily, "Look at what that
bloody dog has done," as he picked it up with his
fingers, dusted it off with his sleeve and put it in
his pocket.

Really, I would like to have spent a couple of hours
in the front room with Jen, but unfortunately their
house was crowded what with a boy evacuee and lodger
war-worker, Mr Stacey. At that time there was no spare
room to stay the night, let alone take over the front
room for a couple of hours.

Like all holidays, the remaining leave flew by. I, of
course, had to visit my old workmates at Skurray's
Garage (those who had not joined up). Besides private
work, they had WD (War Department) vehicles and a
couple of hundred soldiers on vehicle maintenance
courses. These courses and WD work were in operation
before I joined the Navy. I had attended the
three-month course, so was interested to see how they
had progressed. I thought that some of the instructors
were digging themselves in for good jobs for after the

war. Never mind, I must have enjoyed my naval life or I wouldn't have started this tale.

I had just two more days left of my leave — even the thought of leaving made my heart heave, and Jennie was feeling just the same. This time I was not going far — just across the Channel. Some blokes had even swum that distance! We just wanted a slice of luck with us and we were sure we would come through it all.

Jennie and I had one more evening left in the front room when a few tears were shed, and then one of us came up with a bright idea — let's get engaged! There was no time left to have a party or tell anyone, or even buy a ring. This would just have to wait until the next leave.

For an extra bit of fun, why not ask Jennie to come up to London with me tomorrow and meet some of the boys? It would also mean another few hours together, which was great, but would Jennie be OK travelling back on the train on her own? Of course she would be OK, but I'd better not let her Dad know! That's settled then. We let my parents know that Jennie was coming to London with me. They were both OK, although Mum "tutted" a bit and Dad look a bit worried and said, "Now, be careful, son. Don't let anything happen to her."

So, the next morning we indulged in the luxury of hiring a taxi to take us to the station. The train was packed and we had to stand in the corridor — luckily, the corridor was not so crowded. Just before Reading I went into the toilet, and on opening the door the handle and spindle came away in my hand. It was a good job the handle did not fall outside the door, or else I would have been locked in the lav! On coming out, I put the handle and spindle back on the door and told Jen what had happened. A little later a middle-aged man went into the loo and I whispered to Jen, "Shall I?" She nodded, so I silently slid the door handle and spindle out of the lock. After a short wait the door started to rattle. I left it and soon the captive started knocking the door and shouting, "Help!" We both laughed and I noisily put the handle and spindle back and opened the door to see a red-faced man waiting. I said, "We heard you banging. The door handle had fallen out. A good job we were outside!" He looked chuffed and said, "Thanks a lot, mate. I've got to get off at Reading." When he got off, Jennie and I both had a good laugh. It helped to break the gloom, knowing that this journey was the start of another parting.

Arriving at Paddington Station there was a crowd of about a dozen sailors milling about on the platform. "There they are," I said, as I picked out the faces of the lads I knew so well. We went over to them. "Howdy, mates. Back again. This is Jennie," as I introduced them to Jen. "This is Raggy Rex. This is Les Greenaway. This is . . ." and so on.

We had to hang around for about an hour or so, which was difficult, knowing we would be parting soon. After crossing London, Jennie saw our train off at Kings Cross, and we waved until we were out of sight. The return journey to Harwich went without a hitch and it seemed no time before we were back on the old 406, as if the 14 days' leave had not happened. In a few days I received a letter from Jen telling me how she had arrived back in Swindon OK, and how much she had enjoyed London.

Back on board again everything seemed to be buzzing — groups of seamen with their bell bottoms turned up, some with blue overalls, cleaning everything in sight and painting everything grey or white. If this was a coal ship I swear they would even have painted the coal. There were "miles" of thick rope to be rolled up and heaving lines to be rolled and stowed away, like sailors do. The gunnery ratings stripped and cleaned the six Oerlikon guns, and the 12-pounder was stripped down and laid out on the upper deck looking like a large jigsaw puzzle. I hoped PO Penn knew how to put it back together!

Down below gangs of stokers were working on the three diesel generators, cleaning and changing fuel filters and the generators' oil filters and filling the engines with new oil. Now what else was there to check? There was the refrigeration plant, auxiliary boiler, ballast pumps, fire and bilge pumps, elevator winch, boat winches, ramp motor, bow door motor, anchor and Kedge anchor winches, not forgetting the galley equipment. It was almost like keeping a small town running. I nearly forgot, the Engineer Officer had to make sure he ordered engine fuel and fresh water which would all be delivered by tankers and put into the correct tanks — it wouldn't be right to have to cancel D-Day because someone forgot to order the fuel! What was I doing amongst all that lot? I dunno —

probably just running around like a "blue ass fly", like the rest of the crew.

During the next few weeks everyone was very busy and those of the crew who stayed back when we went on leave were sent home rejoicing for the next two weeks. Later a working party from the shore base came aboard to fit a barrage balloon on the forward deck and also equipment to make smoke. Of course, to man the extra equipment about eight new crew members arrived and I had one new motor mechanic and a couple of stokers to make up the numbers in the engineering crew.

Harwich now seemed very crowded with landing craft and strange craft like LSTs with their top decks filled with rocket launchers, and there were plenty of craft with fresh troops doing some training. It was during this time that one of these exercises was to become notorious. It was named exercise Tiger, with a make-up of eight US LSTs. In the early hours of 28th April 1944 these LSTs, fully loaded with US troops, left Lyme Bay and came under attack from E-boats. US LST 507 was torpedoed and sank with the loss of 282 troops, and US LST 531 was sunk with the loss of 424 men. US LST 289 was victim of another torpedo, but she managed to limp to Dartmouth with four of her crew dead and eight others missing, presumed dead. This was upsetting at the time, but they were not ships that we had sailed with — US LSTs usually sailed with their own flotillas and at that time we had just come back from Italy and were hardened to losing ships. We were, of course, shattered at the loss of so many men on an exercise but had to forget about it as soon as possible. After the war a memorial was erected on the beach at Slapton Sands in Devon.

During the end of May and early June all our minds were focused on the coming invasion, and even though we had been through it all before, everyone was on tenterhooks. In my mind we had got away with the Italian campaign lightly; at least the 406 did. We must have had Lady Luck with us because there were thousands of men and women who had one hell of a war. For us it was a question of being in the right place at the right time and missing all the shells and nasties that Jerry had thrown at us, and then think of all those US sailors who were killed on the exercise a few weeks before off Slapton Sands. There was a chance that our luck could run out, but on the other hand we now had three first-day landings under our belt. With all that experience around us we should be able to get through with as good a chance as anyone.

Because of very rough seas and high winds the original D-Day date was postponed for 24 hours. The 7th LST flotilla left Parkestone Quay, Harwich on the afternoon of 5th June. There were many hours of sailing ahead of us before joining our counterparts from ports on the south coast, and then the long awaited D-Day landings, or as known by the rest of the world, the Second Front. It was only in later years that I discovered the official name of the operation was Overlord.

Dockyard workers, shore staff and crowds of ordinary workers and mums and dads lined the dockyard roads and shore, waving and cheering, especially when our little flotilla broke our battle ensigns. There was no doubt that this was the Big One. To the crew and also the troops on board, we were now in the hands of battle-hardened veterans, some all of 20 years old, but I'm sure few, if any, would have wished to be anywhere else. Most felt dry in the mouth with stomach muscles tightened, but everyone felt they had to see it through.

When we reached Portsmouth, everywhere was very calm; the bulk of the invasion fleet had not met up. We sailed into the harbour to pick up several war correspondents. Even here there were crowds of people to wave and cheer. We were soon on our way again and everyone was checking and rechecking; no one wanted a cock-up. As darkness fell, everyone seemed to be talking in a whisper. No doubt Hollywood might one day make a film about all this with the "Star-spangled banner" blaring out, bugles blowing and flags waving — but it was not like that.

There was a feeling of secrecy all about us as we put our trust in silence and stealth. As the night moved slowly on, I went into the signal cabin to find out if there was anything happening. No news was good news. Just before dawn "Action Stations" was piped, and everyone moved to their allotted stations. The cooks were busy making and wrapping sandwiches, just in case they would be needed. I know I managed to scrounge a steaming hot mug of cocoa — that went down really well. All the gun crews were at their posts and keeping a good lookout for E-Boats and torpedo tracks. Now dawn was upon us.

It was then that a cacophony of sound broke out. Heavy guns fired from battleships and cruisers — the boom and crack of the smaller cannons and bombs exploding inland, dropped by the RAF. There was also a new noise which we had not heard in Italy, an ear-piercing scream of rockets launched from the upper deck of rocket-carrying LSTs. When dawn really broke we were treated to an amazing sight. There were thousands of ships of all shapes and sizes as far as the eye could see, and the noise was deafening even though we were still a few miles from the shore. We could also see several old ships being scuttled just off the shore to make a breakwater for the landing beach.

Everything appeared to be going well and the beach was now looming closer, but there were no shell explosions on the beach or in the sea. There were tanks, trucks and troops all over the beach as far as the eye could see, so we could guess the initial attack had gone well. The troops aboard had all disappeared into their various tanks and trucks. Engines were started and the whole ship had come alive. The Kedge anchor had been dropped, the tide was high and everyone and everything was ready for our first landing in France.

Action Stations were in operation and we all moved to our stations. I was in the main engine room with two stokers, Bill Porter and George White and Motor Mechanic PO Les Greenaway. Of course, there was also the Engineer Officer, complete with his belt and revolver. We thought nothing of this, but wondered why, as we closed the watertight doors, locking us all in the engine room.

The beaching went well, we could feel the sand scraping the bottom beneath our feet and the 406 was coming to a halt, just as she did when we ran aground on the Clyde several years before. We could hear and feel the bow doors opening and the rumble of the tanks as they tentatively moved down the ramp onto the sandy beach. It wasn't long before dozens of LSTs were on the beach spewing out tanks and trucks onto the now crowded beach. The initial drive off the ramps had to be taken very cautiously for mine clearance was still in its first stage. By the time unloading had been completed the tide was out, so the 406 was high and dry. It was quite a sight to see large ships — dozens of them — dried out about two hundred yards up the beach. It was possible to walk right around the ships and touch the propellers.

The first day was passing very quickly; there had been little enemy activity. There was, of course, loads of wreckage scattered all over the very large beach and debris floating in the sea — wreckage of several LCTs that had struck mines or had received hits from shells on the initial run in. The beach parties, which included the Army and Naval ratings, had set up camps and were helping the beach marshals to sort out the confusion, as more and more troops and heavy equipment arrived. By now there was no enemy activity to talk about. To our minds, the landings had gone well on the British and Canadian beaches, which had been named Gold, Juno and Sword. American beaches were Utah and

Omaha. These names have been etched into the minds of all those men who spent only a day or two on these beaches.

By now we had heard that the American Army had received severe casualties on Utah. The beach was very steep and rocky and at the end were cliffs. Hundreds were lost trying to scramble up the beach and over the rocks, with the enemy firing from the high ground.

Even though there was very little enemy activity, the sooner we pulled off the better. The Kedge anchor held fast and the tide was well in, so we were soon afloat and on our way back to England to load up once again. The night was now dark and the wind strong, and the sea was very choppy. We were all feeling on a high, with the expectation that the German Navy would be waiting with gunboats and U-boats to take their revenge. Luckily, none of this materialised, for the Royal Navy was looking after its own, and we were soon safely back in our own waters.

We were part of a shuttle service working between ports in the south of England and the Normandy beaches — loading with hardware and ammunition at Southampton for the two armies slogging their way into France, and to transport back to England the wounded and maybe prisoners of war. This time we loaded with Bren carriers and Canadian troops and also a number of Bedford S-type trucks loaded with food. During the journey back the next morning we were all wondering what several LSTs and tug boats were towing to Normandy. It appeared to be large steel or concrete tanks or floating rafts. Whatever it was, we were sure we would find out soon enough.

The weather in the Channel was still very changeable and very windy, and a rough, choppy sea did not help the troops digging in on the beaches. However, it wasn't long before we were in the Normandy area once again preparing to beach. We were all now proficient at beaching. The Kedge anchor had to be dropped at the correct time, the ship travelling at the correct speed. The beach marshal was flagging us in and everyone was at standby. The anchor had been dropped and we were in about ten feet of water when we hit and scraped an object below us. A screeching noise and crunching could be heard from under our feet, but it was too late to stop. So, onward we went, right up the beach — luckily it wasn't a mine or I wouldn't be here to tell the tale!

Everything had to carry on, and unloading started. When completed, a check of the lower plates was carried out. It was found to be a tear about three or four feet long in the bottom plates, just under the main engine room. On pumping out the bilges the tear could be seen, with sand that was pushed into the bilge space when we slid onto the beach. We had to wait for several hours until the tide went out and left the 406 high and dry. The ship was standing very stable on a dry beach and the rip in the plate was held off the beach about four feet high held up by the propeller guards and the two rudder guards. There was about three feet between the damage and the sand, so repairs could be carried out . . . if we could find a Navy or Army group who had welding gear at their, or our, disposal. Our Engineer Officer rang around and contacted an Army workshop set up on the beach and they agreed to take on the work. Our boys dug out the sand underneath the damage, which left plenty of room to weld a plate over the top.

Meanwhile, a group of our lads waded into the sea where the accident happened and soon found the cause — it was a British tank that had been hit during the first day and had sunk into the sand and was covered by the sea. The tide came in and unfortunately it was not discovered until we ran over it. There were no bodies in the tank so we reckoned the crew got away with it OK.

Owing to the damage we could not journey back until late the next day. We spent part of this day lazing on the beach, hoping the enemy did not start a counter-attack. I always felt safer on board at sea than having to face the enemy on land. (I often wondered if that made me a bit of a coward, until I spoke to soldiers on board who were most anxious to get back on dry land — quite the opposite to me!)

The repair was carried out satisfactorily and the damaged tank was dug out and removed from the beach, so we were now ready to pull off and resume the shuttle service. We noticed more and more of the aforementioned prefabricated giant water tanks forming up out in the Channel. Over the next couple of weeks we carried out three more journeys back and forwards to England and the mystery prefab "tanks" were now forming into a large prefab harbour. As the time went on, the shape of the harbour could be seen — there were miles of prefab roads, almost like a spider's web, reaching to the beach from several large concrete docks. This meant that LSTs could now unload two or three miles out at sea, onto the "web" of roads. This, of course, took hours off the time taken to unload and reload with homeward cargo, and of course, all the thousands of things needed to sustain the advancing armies. This prefab "wonder harbour", now known as the Mulberry Harbour, contributed greatly to the success of the D-Day Campaign. Unfortunately, the weather deteriorated considerably, with gale force winds, which destroyed the American Mulberry Harbour before it could be used.

We were now loading and returning to Normandy every other day, docking at the Mulberry Harbour and returning to English ports all over the south coast. We were also getting used to shore leave and enjoying what was on offer at the south coast holiday resorts. Of course, this was wartime — the beaches were mined and covered with barbed wire and most of the amusement arcades were closed down. Despite that, there seemed to be plenty to do most evenings and we were getting used to English beer and a glass of rum or gin.

Soon the French ports started to fall to the Allies, and it wasn't long before it was realised that the LST job of beaching to unload was drawing to a close. Large merchant ships were now able to unload in Dieppe, Cherbourg, etc. and some were going into the Dutch and Belgian docks.

Of course, the war in the Far East was still going on and the stories coming back were nearly all bad news — ships and islands being lost and atrocities carried out by the Japanese on the population and prisoners. It wasn't long before a "buzz" came to our ears that the next invasion could possibly be Singapore or Japan herself. We were eventually told that some of the older LSTs, of which we were one, would be going to Clyde, Glasgow for a refit during August, and then onto the Far East in the New Year. What could one say? We were gob smacked. First-day landings at Sicily, Salerno, Anzio and then Normandy, and now this. We thought that the crew and the old 406 had done their bit. We couldn't get a new refit like the 406, but we did think that we were due a cushy number for once.

The shuttle service carried on as usual, although the pressure was now off, so we had some good runs ashore on the Isle of Wight, etc. We used to go out with a group of about six of us, all good mates who had been together — eating, drinking, working, and living together since the birth of the 406. Sometimes we would meet up with a few more of our lads in some bar or other; the drinks would start to flow and then the singing would start up. Some of the songs were beyond par — they all were, if I remember rightly, for even today I can remember the words. Everyone seemed to be having fun and were happy, except one or two of the older married blokes who had received "Dear John letters" from their wives. There was never a real falling-out or a fistfight amongst the crew, for everyone seemed to be looking after each other. Of course, there were plenty of young girls around, but no one seemed to be getting serious — it was always just a good laugh.

Scottish Refit

It was early August and we were now ready to sail to Scotland — look out the Clyde! We were now older and wiser than the last time we were there and stuck in the mud! In a couple of days we were docking in a shipyard in the heart of Glasgow, watching and hearing all the work going on in this great ship building area. Opposite the yard, across the Clyde, was a busy street of rundown shops and pubs and small cafés — we all said, "This'll do us for a couple of months."

It was only a few days before we were moved into dry dock. We first entered the dock and were wedged in with large poles and planks, and then the sea water was pumped out, leaving us high and dry in what seemed a massive hole with steps built all round. The ship was held up very firmly with poles and scaffolding, and large numbers of workmen descended upon us, electricity and water being laid on. All of the crew were detailed to certain duties — some cleaning, some helping the "dockyard maties" and some, as usual, painting.

The dockyard workers stripped down the generators and motors and some of them carried out small repairs to the main engines while we stood by to help out and advise where certain parts were kept. Some of the crew were sent on embarkation leave.

It was during this time that we came across a large wooden crate in one of the spare cabins on the same deck as our workshop. This cabin was never used, and Les and I were only in there to check the main engine exhaust which went through the bulkhead on its way to the engine room. I asked Les what was in the box, but he just replied, "I don't know — shall we have a look?" "Tell you what," I replied, "Let's leave it for a couple of weeks. We'll be in Glasgow for quite a while now and we can keep an eye on it. If it's still here in a couple of weeks we'll open it up."

The days went by and I forgot about the crate, until one day just after we'd had our tot Les said, "What about the box, then?" "Bloody hell," I replied, "I'd forgot all about that — let's go and have a look while everything is quiet." So off we went and found the box still there. "We want a crowbar, hammer and a pair of pliers ... I'll pop down to the workshop," I volunteered. I was soon back with the tools and it didn't take a couple of minutes to ease off the wooden cover, secured by four two-inch nails.

Inside were fistfuls of scrunched-up newspaper, no doubt protecting the contents. It took about half an hour to unload the crate, which turned out to be a complete dinner service. Everything was there for a full-scale dinner: side plates, dinner plates, vegetable dishes, soup bowls, and all of high-quality white china. One could imagine it looking very elegant set on a wardroom table — it must have been worth a bomb, especially now there was a war on as things like that were in short supply.

"What do you think this little lot is worth?" said Les, "Twenty . . . thirty . . . fifty pounds? We ought to get at least £15 for this lot. Let's get the boys together and set about shifting it. It's going to be salted away unless we do something about it . . . so let's salt it away ourselves!"

I mustered four oppos to come at seven o'clock but to meet on the stern deck at six o'clock for the full know-how. I had a large buffalo-hide suitcase in which we lovingly placed all the pieces, wrapped carefully in newspaper for safety. The case weighed about half-a-hundredweight and it was no easy task passing through Customs and sauntering out of the dockyard trying to look as natural as if we were carrying soap, flannels and towels!

In the first pub where we were not known, it was pints all round before casually chatting to the landlord. After a couple of minutes we were round the back showing him our wares. All was going well until the landlord noticed the blue anchor stamped on the bottom of every piece of china, bringing our negotiations to an abrupt end. "Hey, I can't buy this lot — it belongs to the 'Andrew' . . . you'd better move it quick."

The conversation was the same in the next three pubs, by which time we had all downed four pints apiece. We had all taken a turn in lugging the heavy suitcase round the dark, cold streets and we were fed up to the back teeth. The cost of the beer and the indignity of being turned away from all the pubs without making a sale was the end. "What are we going to do now?" said one of my mates, "We can't very well take it back on board."

We were just passing the dry dock when we all had the same thought. Yes, we opened the case once again and very gingerly walked to the edge of the dark, dry dock. Looking down about 30-40 feet, the bottom was awash with black water, mud and gunge. Two of us caught hold of the handles at each end of the case and with one heave the whole lot disappeared into the black hole with an almighty crash and bang, never to be seen again . . . we hoped. Four chastened men then disappeared into the bowels of the 406 not to be seen again until six o'clock the next morning when we all fell in on the upper deck to start our day's work.

As soon as we could, we met up and lined the guard rail, peering into the dry dock to make sure all the evidence had disappeared. But what met our eyes? One seaman, a Welshman called Pete, was slopping about in the gunge at the bottom of the dry dock. "What's that silly sod doing down there?" was the comment voiced. "What you doing down there, Taffy?" we shouted down to him. "Oh," he shouted back, "I was a bit worse for wear last night and puked up over the side, but my blasted teeth went over as well — I reckon they're gone forever."

That, I think, was the last of the "dinner set affair". I don't know if Taffy ever did get his teeth back, and I don't think the dinner service was found either.

It took two or three weeks to settle into a new mode of living. Our home (ship) was now crowded with strangers who had infiltrated into all our hide-away places, the main and generator engine rooms, to the paint and cable lockers and prop shaft tunnel. All these places seemed to be uprooted and we, the crew, had to try to hide out of sight and out of mind.

Even our everyday living altered. Half of the crew, including officers, were away on leave, so the rest of us were trying to look busy. Most days we managed to go into Glasgow to buy a few rabbits, disappearing into a bar for a few drinks and a bite or two. We eventually started to use the pub opposite our shipyard, just in sight of the 406. I cannot remember the name of the pub, but it turned out to be good, warm and clean. The landlord and his lady were very friendly, and his midday meals were quite good for the price — usually a home-made pork pie, ham sandwich, or bread and cheese. Every day at about 12.30 we noticed rows of pints of beer were lined up along the bar, each accompanied by a glass of Scotch whisky — awaiting the dockyard maties, who swarmed in at lunchtime.

It was noticeable that in a far corner sat a lonely old lady at a round table. On the table was a metal box, a book, and a large glass of whisky or gin. The lady was dressed all in black, complete with a black shawl, bonnet and long lace-up boots. During the dinner hour lots of the dockyard workers would queue up at her table to pay her money; she would open her box with a key tied to her wrist with real ribbon, and enter some figures into her book. We eventually got to know this

114

sweet old lady. Her name was Rosie, and she was the local moneylender. She was a great character and thought the world of us lads, often sending whisky over to our table. We found out later that she was a millionaire who lived by herself in a large old house nearby. At least that was what we were told!

After a week or so, we got to know a lot of the locals and they found out that we had taken part in the Italian landings and also had just finished with the D-Day landings. As you can imagine, to have a large landing ship based opposite and the crew "almost locals", their imaginations were excited and we could do nothing wrong, much to our embarrassment. Drinks came in from all angles — great lads, these dockyard maties!

The days and weeks soon passed and by the middle of September the ship's overhaul was almost complete. The 19th September was my birthday, so I had to look forward to a special dinner and "sippers" all round from the engine room ratings. All well and good; that's if everything turns out as it should. Does it ever? By 7 o' clock everything was going swimmingly — by 7.30 I must have been flat out. I can't remember the birthday dinner — in fact, I can't remember anything until about 9 o'clock the next morning. Great birthday that was! I couldn't take rum for about two months after that lot — never again . . . perhaps!

After the refit we were on sea trials, making sure everything was spot on for the 8,000 mile journey, and possibly three or four landings ahead of us. By now we knew most of the weak parts of the workings of the LST and made sure we were on top of any mishap that might happen. The days were flying past now. We had been told that we would be off to the Far East in January. There were fourteen days' embarkation leave to get in and then move up the Clyde to have a large LCI (Landing Craft Infantry) fitted to the top deck. This craft must have weighed at least a thousand or two tons and would no doubt make the old 406 top-heavy — well, they said it was safe, so be it!

Time had now come for home leave. I was loaded up once again with Christmas presents, dressed in a blue suit and greatcoat, for it was now getting cold out in the wide world. In the breast pocket of my greatcoat was a flat half-bottle of Pussers Rum, especially for Dad. The train soon arrived and I was in a carriage with a couple of sailors, but as the light was drawing in, I closed my eyes and was soon asleep. It seemed only a couple of minutes before we stopped at Manchester — "All change for London." I soon pulled myself together and found myself on a platform in Manchester waiting for the London train.

I was feeling tired and bored when I noticed a young lady about to pass me. As she did so, she stopped walking, put her hands to her eyes and then keeled over, falling heavily onto her back. I was, of course, soon woken up and rushed to her assistance. I lifted her head and could see that she was out cold. Soon another sailor turned up and asked if he could help. It could be seen that a doctor or First Aid man was required. I thought of that bottle in my coat pocket — would rum bring her round, or make her worse? Luckily, a First Aid man turned up and she was whisked away into a warm waiting room. We were soon told that she had come round and would probably be OK.

It appeared that the train pulling into the station was ours, so we found our way into an empty carriage, stowing our luggage and making ourselves comfortable. Me and this other sailor were like real "oppos" now, no doubt because we had both gone to the rescue of the girl in distress. It then came to me that the bottle of Dad's rum was still in my pocket, as I had not used the "medicine" on the girl. I pulled out the bottle and remarked to my oppo, "Look what I nearly opened — what about a sippers?" He looked delighted. "Hey, is that a drop of Pussers? Yes, please." The cap was soon off the bottle as we sat back and enjoyed the journey through the dark countryside, both talking and laughing between sips of Pussers and coming to the conclusion that life in "The Andrew" wasn't so bad after all.

Within a few hours I found myself standing on Swindon platform with kit bag and suitcase, wondering how I managed to act so sensibly to get out at Swindon with all my belongings intact — may be I was growing up fast and using my loaf. Anyway, I was home now, although I did feel a bit shaky on my legs and I had a job to get my eyes to focus correctly. Crikey! What are Mum and Dad going to say — me going home half-cut after being away fighting the "Ka-Ka Germans"? This is what brother Dick used to call the Germans when Dad was away in France in the 1914 war. On the platform was a tea trolley, manned by a Salvationist and I obtained a free cup of tea. I drank the tea and hung about the station for about an hour to make sure I had sobered up and then slowly walked the mile home.

I think the excitement of being home sobered me up more than anything, and it wasn't long before I was sat in my chair around the table eating sausages, mash and tinned tomatoes. There were happy faces all round the table, and although I was now tired out, we didn't get our heads down until about one o'clock in the morning.

The fourteen days' leave was great, but went by like a flash. Jen and I visited everyone we should — aunts and uncles, old friends and new friends of Jennie's, and I even visited Skurray's to find out who was still working there and who had joined up. We went to the pictures, the Savoy and the Regent, and went out for drinks with Dick and Grace — Dick was also home on leave so it was good to go over old times and talk of our meeting in the desert when we were in Tripoli.

Swindon had not changed a lot since I had been away, but there were one or two new restaurants opening up so the four of us went out for a meal, which was quite a new experience in those days. It was The Violet Café in Old Town, and Jen reminds me that someone spilt the salt and that we were all in hysterics trying to cover it up, not being used to going out for meals!

The one thing I missed was Swindon Town Football Club, which seemed to have closed for the duration of the war. The home of the Third Division South football team was the County Ground, just across the road from my home — we could even see the ball if it was kicked high enough, or if we stood on a chair in the front bedroom window. We had an average pro team, always halfway up or down the Third Division, but we always thought that one day we would be going up . . . even to the dizzy heights of the First Division. We now had to hope that one day we would have a team again, but of course the war had to be won before that could happen. I guess these were the thoughts that pushed us forward during this time.

The last leave was now over — we didn't have time to do anything to write about, but I know we all enjoyed it, even though the thought of going to the Far East was looming.

On the last day of my leave Jennie and I went into town, just wasting time, talking and walking and trying to look into the future — even this was impossible in those days. The evening was spent in the County Hotel just across the road from home and was, of course, Dad's and our "local". We had a great night — Dick and Grace, Jennie, myself and several "old timers". It was a pity Mother wouldn't come (she wouldn't be seen in a public bar for all the money in the world), and of course, Brian was too young to go out drinking. Mother was at home getting supper ready. Dad finished off the rum that I handed over the first day home, and of course I had to apologise for why there was only a little bit left. I don't think Dad liked the rum very much for it was very strong and one needed to get used to taking "gulpers" before you could enjoy it. Anyway, I had a good send-off.

I left home for Glasgow about nine o'clock in the morning. It was very cold and cloudy and the light was gloomy, just like we all felt. Jennie could not come back with me as she did before, as the trains had been re-routed. I had to change at Oxford, but eventually arrived back in Glasgow late in the evening. I went to the RPO, who soon arranged for the RN to let me know where the 406 was now docked; it turned out that she was still in the same dock she was in when I went on leave. I soon got a taxi and was back on board in less than half an hour.

Everything was back to normal; Jennie was in Swindon, I was back on the 406 — and the war was still on. I was beginning to wonder what was normal now. While I was on leave the refit had been finished. All that remained was sea trials and then the fitting of the LCI onto the upper deck. It took several weeks before we really were ready for sea trials, but the time did eventually arrive.

My first morning started by sorting out my living space. The locker was OK, everything was intact and all my writing kit was as I had left it — ready to start my letter writing to Jen again. My lovely moleskin square rig suit was hung up after giving it a good brushing and ironing. Most of my laundering had been done at home, but I did have a couple of shirts and a sheet that would have to be washed and ironed.

I now had to spend a few hours with the boss man, hearing how good or bad the refit had been. I went to the engineer's cabin after lunch and "tot" time, and spent about three hours hearing about the rough time he'd had with the dockyard engineers, etc — I was not at all surprised, but I did sympathise with him after three neat whiskies.

The next couple of days I spent going around the ship with Cliff Hensby, the ERA, starting the generators and main engine. As far as we could tell, everything was OK and, no doubt, sea trials would soon sort out any adjustments or unforeseen faults. After taking on fuel, oil and fresh water, it was arranged to carry out trials on the Thursday; it would take a couple of days if everything went well. On the day, three dockyard engineers, the RN engineer, and two of our own crew, Cliff Hensby and myself, had to stand by, although we were only there to answer questions and fetch and carry.

The two-day trials went off OK; in fact it was enjoyable, and also an eye-opener. The dockyard engineers knew their job. I, at least, was impressed and felt more at ease about undertaking the journey to the Far East with the heavy LCI attached to the upper deck. Now that the trials had proved OK, we were moved into a deep-water dock next to a large crane. The LCI and all the gear was waiting for work to start on loading the upper deck.

The next morning, after a breakfast of bacon, eggs and fried bread, we mustered on the deck to help load and fit the LCI, which was destined for the Far East, on our upper deck. There were six great wooden beams already cut to size that had to be laid out across the deck. Of course, the dockyard team had plans and measurements where everything fitted. It was paramount that the great weight was set in its correct position or else it was possible that the 406 could capsize in heavy seas.

Eventually, the fitters were satisfied, and the beams were greased and fitted and bolted to the deck. The huge cranes then lifted the LCI onto its mounting, and heavy chains were bolted to the beams. The LCI chains also had adjusting bolts, which could be tightened if they became loose at sea. It all looked safe and sound, but we were putting our faith in the hands of the dockyard fitters. We were a bit concerned how we would get the LCI "off our backs" when we arrived at our destination. It was explained that a list of about 20° would be put on the 406, and explosive charges would break the chains. The LCI would then slide from the greased mountings, sideways into the sea . . . or so we hoped!

By now Christmas had come and gone and the usual things happened — decorating the mess, sending presents and cards to all, and making sure we had plenty of Nelson's Blood (rum) to see us over Christmas. We all enjoyed the Christmas — not quite as we would have at home, but then there was a war on. We did enjoy time spent in our "local", the pub with our Rosie moneylender. Most of the crew joined in with the singing and merry-making, and the beer and spirits flowed. New Year's Day, a Scottish holiday, was our last chance for a "run ashore" before we left for our long journey to the Far East.

Six of the engineering staff — Les, Fred, Micky, Ted, Cliff and, of course, yours truly — decided it was time we gave the city of Glasgow the "once over". We tried several watering holes and by about 10 o'clock we went into a rather posh-looking bar — more like a cocktail bar than the usual four-ale bar frequented by matalots. We all ordered pints of beer, but after a few sips we began to notice something was not quite right. Most of the male customers were wearing lipstick and eye-shadow. One very noticeable was a Lt Commander (RN). He wore his cap, complete with gold braid, on the back of his head with his blond hair swept upwards to the peaked cap. When one of our crowd accidentally knocked his arm and spilt beer on his sleeve, in a lisping falsetto voice he squeaked, "Hey, mind my cloak," and he flicked his fingers over his sleeve. We had to get out of this place fast for we were all in hysterics and would have ended up in trouble with an RN Commander if we were not careful — who would believe us pirates against an RN poofter?

The night went well, until we were told of a dance in a large building just across the road from wherever we were. The dance was up three flights of concrete stairs, with a large wooden door right at the top — the door had a sliding grill, which slid open about an inch when we kicked the door. "Whadya want?" said a gruff Scottish voice. One of us replied, "We've come to the dance." The grunt said, "Are you Catholic?" Before we could answer there was a rumpus behind the door, which suddenly burst open and two bouncers the size of a bus manhandled a little bloke through the door and bundled him down the concrete stairs. Cripes! We didn't want any of that — we were on holiday. We turned and followed the poor bloke down the stairs, laughing and singing. We then had to find our way back to the old 406, safe and sound, with a successful night out in the city under our belts and plenty of tales to tell.

The holiday period was now over and we all seemed to settle down to a humdrum life for the next few weeks. We did arrange a couple of football matches against a couple of LST teams. I remember one was LST 401, whom we beat 2-0 . . . at least I think we did! Life at this time was very easy on board and on shore — it was as if we were on standby waiting for it all to happen. On board it was make-and-mend and cleaning, or housework if you like — eating, sleeping, writing letters, and to keep us as fit and supple as we should be, was football, cross-country running and boxing. Unfortunately, we did not have any real sports equipment, but we had been promised that some would arrive onboard one day; that, however, is another story.

The Far East

The day arrived for us to leave Glasgow, and on 30th June we dropped anchor at Greenock to await the arrival of five other LSTs of our flotilla. Only two arrived, and the next day we sailed to Liverpool to meet up with the rest of our convoy to Gibraltar. The convoy was made up of 18 vessels and five LSTs — 406, 410, 415, 427 and 538 — and three escorts, but we had to wait about for four days before we eventually gathered all the ships together and set sail for Gibraltar.

The weather had now turned very rough and it was the first time we had sailed any distance with the LCI on the upper deck. To put it mildly, our LST behaved a little better when in a beam-on sea — no doubt the extra weight helped to quieten the excessive vibration when the prop shafts came out of the water. It was frightening in a side-on sea, as the roll was very bad and slow. Many a night I lay in my bunk when a heavy roll was on; the 406 would roll slowly to the port side and would appear to stay there. "Get up! Get up, you bastard!" I would murmur as I rolled onto my left side, then she would slowly right herself. Then it would happen again on the starboard side. Was I going to be sick, or would she continue her roll and slide slowly under the cruel sea? As I felt just then, I don't think I would have minded.

To make matters more frightening, was the noise coming from the upper deck — breaking, cracking and heavy bumping, as the holding chains rolled and twisted as the heavy load tried to break free. I know that if the LCI did break free, she would slide over the upper deck taking everything that got in her way into the sea.

The journey to Gibraltar was a nightmare. The weather was wild and the wind blew at gale force for five days. We were all in a state of worry about the safety of the cargo and wondering if the chains were strong enough to hold fast in such heavy weather. The rolling, bucking and the gale made it impossible to go out on the upper deck to examine the chains and the lashings. We just had to hope and pray that everything was still secure.

On top of all this I think my biggest worry was the two main engines that had been screaming away day after day. Was it possible they would last? If they packed up now we would all be lost. I know my hearing had adjusted to every strange noise coming from those engines, and every time I woke up when at sea my first thought was, "Good, those engines sound OK."

On 9th February 1945, we arrived at Gibraltar. The sea had calmed down and the sun was shining; in fact, it was a perfect summer's day. There were lots of ships, both merchant and RN ships, like us, still involved in the war which was continuing on in Europe and also in the Far East and Burma.

It wasn't long before we were alongside in the harbour. In less than an hour, the port watch was ready to go ashore. It wasn't far to walk to the RN barracks and then to the POs' mess. After nine days of horrendous rolling, it felt as if we were still at sea, or maybe had just drunk three neat rums, when we walked only a short way to the POs' mess. The POs mess at Gibraltar was very good. But then, most RN messes dotted around the world are always pristine — spotlessly clean, brass work sparkling, billiard tables, dart boards . . . everything hard-pressed sailors needed.

During our nine days at Gibraltar we played tombola and partook of a few English beers most evenings. Afternoons were spent, when not working on board, frequenting street cafés and watering holes. One afternoon a dozen of us walked halfway up the Rock, a rough rocky road, to see the apes of Gibraltar. True to form, they were all there, so it seemed the British Empire was still safe, at least for a few more years. The saying goes, "When the apes leave Gibraltar, Britain will lose her Empire!"

Within a couple of days LST 428 arrived and tied up alongside of us, and unloaded a medium-sized sailing boat — maybe the skipper had bought this for after the war. During the day the rest of our flotilla arrived to pick up provisions, and all the skippers went ashore for further orders (so we guessed). The next day all of the LSTs, including us, set off on our journey. Next stop, Port Said.

The journey to Port Said was not good — the weather had deteriorated and the dreaded rolling had started again. We anchored off Port Said on 26th February, after nine days of bad weather. It was noticed that the weather was now hotting up. The sea had flattened out and we were able to get ashore by liberty boat — so we had a day ashore in front of us in Port Said.

Port Said was a typical town of the Middle East — crowded streets and roads, thousands of flies and mozzies, and of course the usual excess of native vendors selling their wares from baskets or trays hung around their person, and pushing their faces and wares into one, shouting, "Buy dirty pictures, etc., buy fruit or cigs, Johnny!" Walking through the crowds we would reply, "No thanks, no thanks. Maybe tomorrow, no, no, bugger off! Get lost!" yet I think I did purchase a pineapple and some horrible sweets (talk about vulnerable British sailors ashore in foreign climes).

The next day we left this wondrous town for the Suez Canal. The canal was just as I'd imagined it: sand dunes, palm trees and several very old buildings along both sides, and every now and again a posse of police would ride by on camels with long old-fashioned rifles slung around their backs. It took us about nine hours to travel the whole length and then to anchor in the wide holding area at the mouth of the canal. Here the rest of our squadron mustered for three days and we only went ashore in Port Suez on duty.

The weather was now good but not as hot as we had expected — no doubt we would regret saying that. Our stay at Port Suez had now reached eight days, and we were getting a bit edgy at staying around doing nothing. That day the skipper cleared the lower deck and announced that tomorrow we would be sailing for Cochin in south west India — this would be a long trip, possibly fourteen days. By now the weather was improving and we were hoping that we would not have to put up with rolling for two or three weeks.

We did sail the next day. The five LSTs went off together and in a few hours the land disappeared — a large sea, the Red Sea, took its place. It was 8th March 1945 when our small convoy of five LSTs set sail for Cochin. Hot weather had arrived and looked set for the duration — it was perfect. The 406 was ploughing on and on at about ten knots day after day without sight of land. In fact it could have been a holiday cruise. If it was, we didn't know what was at the end of it. We soon passed into the Gulf of Aden and then into the Indian Ocean, which had become so calm it looked as if dust was covering the whole of the vast expanse of water. I believe they call it "plankton" but it looked like dust to me.

The shimmering waves caused by our large bow doors ploughing through the calm sea sent dozens of flying fish darting outwards like living spray; quite a lot even landed on the deck. For me this part of the long sea journey was breathtaking and was even improved when we were honoured with a display of diving and leaping by a school of whales. We had lots of days like this and another eight days before we sighted land, and it wasn't long before we were entering the mouth of a river and then into the harbour of Cochin.

We proceeded very slowly to eventually dock alongside rows of palm trees and what looked like native houses and shops, and a long, low building flying the "white duster", which we knew must be a Royal Navy building. At first sight, like a pantomime setting, one expected to see Robinson Crusoe any minute. It was good to shut down the engines and give our ears a rest from the continual roar and to go ashore and enjoy a native village, and of course a beverage or two of the local brew.

Cochin turned out to be a Royal Navy base and several Government buildings were dotted about, which meant that there were lots of RN lads and lassies. This in turn meant that there must be some good canteens and leisure facilities to be found.

There were dozens of "bum boats" flocking around the LSTs, all "chock-a-block" with bananas, pineapples and water melons for sale. It had taken 14 days to reach Cochin, so we were all ready for a run ashore in our well-pressed whites, looking and feeling like ice-cream men. As we were now in India, a large part of the British Empire, we had to smarten ourselves up and try not to look like pirates, and to keep the Union flag flying.

Cochin was a big Royal Navy base where lots of British government persons worked. Lots of the natives could speak English and the majority were very friendly. The first night ashore a crowd of us decided to try out the beer in the Hotel Terminus which looked clean and wholesome   it turned out to be very good, but the weather was so hot we gave up on the beer and tried the gin and tonic with plenty of ice. As this was a well-run hotel the ice was safe to drink. The evening was going very well and Fred was in a singing mood. Even I gave them a rendering of the Old Monk (hope no one knows the words), never to be repeated again.

The next morning it was still very hot and our heads and bodies were feeling the effect of the gin, or whatever some ended up with. So we spent most of the day lounging around the beach and dangling our feet in the sea. The evening was spent playing Tombola and as usual I won nothing. The following day was Good Friday, so we had a lie-in until 7.30 a.m., big deal! In the afternoon we had a challenge from a football team from the RN base — we lost again 3-0. After the match it was into the canteen for a couple of beers and afterwards I managed to smuggle a couple of bottles on board for Fred and Les to help them to recuperate from last night. There was a bit of news when we returned aboard — our new ERA who had been with us for about two months had been sent home on compassionate leave as his wife had been taken ill. His name was Fred Henry and we have never heard from him since.

The next morning most of the seamen were busier than usual for more provisions were brought aboard and had to be stacked away. We were to move on the next morning to Bombay which was a couple of days' sailing. We arrived early morning and tied up next to an old coal-burning tramp steamer. Tied up next to her was a coal barge unloading coal onto the streamer. From the barge were two ladders both fixed at an angle to the top deck and going up the ladders were a line of native women with baskets (filled with coal) balanced on their heads. They went up one ladder and returned empty down the other. The weather was sweltering hot and at the bottom of each ladder were coloured foremen, with a cane which they used on the legs of the women they thought were slacking. The barge was filled with tons and tons of coal that would have taken hours to unload by hand. There was nothing we could do about it. We were, of course, all shocked and were very verbal to the foreman, but someone must have thought trouble was brewing for the 406 was soon moved to a new berth.

Bombay was a large city with a good harbour and most of the crew (including me) had a load of mail from home waiting for us — this always made for a happy ship. I received five letters from Jennie, two from Mum and one from my brother, Dick.

The next day I had to go ashore with the skipper to purchase sports gear for our flotilla, but as he was too busy and could not get a cheque, we had to put this outing off and go a couple of days later. Still, it was worth it, for we had to pick out two complete sets of football shirts and shorts, and four footballs; a set of cricket gear; bats, balls, gloves, and pads, and two sets of boxing gloves — all this gear for each LST in our flotilla. Each set had to be handed over to the LSTs as we met up with them. Guess what happened? We never did meet up with our flotilla again. We were awash with sports gear right up until we were paid off.

Bombay turned out to be a large, colourful, loud city with wide main streets always crowded with people, cows, donkeys, bikes, very old lorries, small and large, but all painted in dazzling colours. Even elephants were painted in bright colours and designs. I mustn't forget the cows, religious icons, wandering wherever they pleased. Believe it or not, I did see a large cow wandering around a very high-class china shop in Bombay, with the Indian shopkeeper trying to make the best of it and not start a stampede — the shopkeeper actually won that time. There were dozens of beggars, both men and women — some had mutilated themselves so they could beg for the "anna". We saw many men with their testicles pierced with a six-inch rusty nail, with an old tin can with a string handle hanging from the nail, to catch the occasional anna tossed by passers-by. There was also the sickening sight of middle-aged men stumping about on gross and obscene legs, swollen from the toes like elephant legs, in pain of suffering from elephantiasis. This terrible disease was almost at epidemic proportions the time we were in Bombay.

The other shocking sights, or should I say, tolerance of British India in that day and age, was the existence of Forrest Road and Grant Road. Both of these roads were out-of-bounds to British servicemen, but four of us from the 406 visited these infamous streets — just to see. Both streets looked like ordinary shopping streets, but by looking just a little harder, you realised that instead of glass there were iron bars in the shop windows and inside were not sweets, fags or clothes, but young and old women, all for sale for a few minutes of their lives. Most of these women and girls had seen their day, their hair was matted and their bodies and faces were tattooed — horrible!

Besides these dregs, other sickening or degrading sights were seen when walking the main streets first thing in the morning. There were large stores and classy stores like the ones seen in Regent Street in London. Most of these shops had deep doorways or porches and every evening the homeless would deposit their bedding and wooden or bamboo bed frames, before settling down for the night. At about 6.30 a.m. the local "gentry" and "ladies" would awaken and proceed to shake their bedding and then bang their bed frames very hard on to the road — we put this down to knocking out the fleas and insects. Very health-conscious, these Asians! There were, however, lots of beautiful buildings and public meeting-places and sports buildings in Bombay.

Almost in the centre of the city was the cricket pavilion and ground, often used when the MCC visited Indian test matches. Also, there was the "Gateway of India", a huge gateway right in the middle of Bombay's sea front. It was here where elegant ladies and gentlemen paraded most evenings, or sat in the sun on wooden carved benches dotted around. The ladies really did look beautiful in their colourful silk saris. A few of us often used to sit under the Gateway, talking and enjoying the sunset and the lovely warm evenings.

That reminds me of one evening like this in the Med when I took my bed on to the upper deck. "Prickly Pearce", a seaman of many years, probably about 40 years old, was on watch on one of the Oerlikon guns just above where I put my bed. He started to cough and suddenly started to swear — "What's up, Prickly?" I shouted to him. "I've just coughed my upper set overboard," he replied — he went right on to his demob at the end of the war without his false teeth. Sorry about that!

I was very sorry to hear that we were soon to leave Bombay for I was getting to like the city which was an education as to the way the Asian people lived. This time our stay in Bombay was short-lived, for the next morning we had to move next to an oil tanker to load oil for our next sailing. The weather had turned a lot cooler and we had a few hours of hard rain. The crew was issued with malaria tablets as the monsoons were about to descend upon us.

We left dock about 1600 hours the next day and set sail for Ceylon, joining a convoy with one escort. The weather had turned hot again and we had three days of heavy rain. During this time our port main engine broke down — this time it was a broken lubricating oil pipe. We put things right in half-an-hour, so we managed to keep up with our convoy. We were now in the Bay of Bengal and it had been raining non-stop for at least six days. We arrived at Trincomalee, Ceylon, at eight o'clock.

There was to be no shore leave, for we were set to sail again the next morning. The skipper cleared the lower deck to say that we were to sail to Kyauru, twenty miles behind the front line in Burma. So dead on time we were off again, this time back into the war zone.

The weather was still hot and the rain had not left off, so instead of getting under the shower every morning, a dozen of us used to go up on the upper deck and let the rain do the cleaning work for us — the rain was lovely and fresh.

It took us five days of sailing to arrive at Kyauru, where the first job was to unleash and launch the LCI which had been fixed to our upper deck for months — it had almost become part of us. The seamen had been working hard from early morning unleashing and removing the wooden sleepers that had held the LCI steady through all the rough weather. An incident, however, marred the final operation. One of the heavy wooden sleepers slipped and smashed four toes on Robby Robinson's left foot. Robby was the best footballer in the 406 team; in fact, he was a pro footballer before he joined the RN. Other than that disaster, the launching went well — it was quite something to see the heavy craft slide into the sea when the charges blew the holding chains. It was quite good to have the whole top deck free and also be able to go into rough weather without the worry of capsizing.

The launching was a great success, so all the seamen and some of the engine room boys set to, with four heavy-duty powerful water hoses, to hose down and clean the upper deck, which hadn't been touched since the LCI — everything went really well until "war" broke out between the seamen cleaners and the stoker cleaners. The power hoses were used as water cannon, bodies were being washed everywhere, one or two even overboard. Everyone, even the officers, let their hair down and great fun and enjoyment was had by all. Kids again. All the tension was gone and a couple of bottles of whisky were unearthed from the wardroom.

After a good night's sleep, we set sail from Kyauru at 10.30 and arrived at Akyab at 5.30 pm. We dropped anchor in the bay for the night and in the morning beached and loaded with troops and equipment. We then pulled off and made for Kyauru where we unloaded the troops that same evening. It had been raining hard for the last 48 hours — about time this monsoon ended!

From the world news it was announced that in Italy the dictator, Mussolini, had been hanged from a lamp post. To us, it seemed that the war in Europe was nearly over. Then, the next day, we had another announcement. Hitler was dead — two down, one to go! With a bit of luck we may be home for Christmas.

With the war going so well, quite a lot of the lads were beginning to get bored and restless. One evening we were lounging in the mess when there was a knock on the door. We all stood up and the skipper with "Jimmy the One" and several hangers-on tramped through the mess, looked around, said goodnight, and continued through into the next room which was for troops when aboard. Now in the deck of this mess was a trap door leading to the main storeroom for things such as barrels of cigarettes, cases of all sorts of spirit: whisky, gin, port and rum. The trap door had a catch locked with an ordinary lock and key through a ring. The whole of the skipper's entourage was down in the Aladdin's cave and the trap door lock and key was lying there waiting. Waiting for someone to fetch a bar of soap and press the key hard into the soap. Someone did this, and it turned out great.

As soon as everyone had settled down, a couple slid down to the engine room workshop, and with the help of a vice, a sharp file and a virgin key, a duplicate key was soon fashioned. We all tiptoed up to the trapdoor, and lo and behold! click — the lock slid open, perfect. Even now I shudder when I think of the risk we were taking — if we had been caught, we would still be behind bars now! Still, what the hell! We had been through three wars and they still sent us out to upset the Japs. Or perhaps it was that we were used to living on our nerves and were getting restless, now that everything was coming to an end.

We left a lookout and we all slid down into the cave. Two buckets were lowered down and filled with bottles of spirit "as required" and enough cigs to last a week or two. All the cases were hammered together to look as if they had not been touched. We were now in the position to have a party when we felt like it — but, watch it, don't get too cocky and drunk! On thinking of this disgraceful episode, it was great fun.

One day we heard that some of the officers' spirits were missing — they were going to search the ship! Now what are we going to do? Shall we dangle the bottles in a paraffin tank — no, they would think of that. What about putting them inside the main engines where there were plates bolted to the crankcase, which could be removed quite quickly. This is where we hid them, and hoped upon hope that we were not ordered to sea. This we did, but we were getting cold feet in case someone noticed that the engine room POs were always in a good mood — it was because we were half-cut!

In the end, we had four bottles of gin left and we decided it would be best if we got rid of these overboard into the "oggin". This we did, and thank heavens they didn't float and follow us into harbour. The next problem was getting rid of the empty bottles for these might float. Great minds said, "Smash them up and throw them overboard into the oggin with the rest." One quiet night alongside in harbour, four buckets filled with broken bottles were sped up to the top deck and then up and over — crash! The motorboat was tied up alongside and was now filled with broken bottles! The next thing to do was convince the powers-that-be that we wanted two stokers to clean out the motorboat, for it was in a disgraceful condition. This is what we did, and I know that I, at least, slept peacefully after that, and the motorboat looked pristine again.

Good news seemed to be coming in everyday now. We had heard that an invasion had been carried out by our forces, just south of Rangoon, and that Rangoon was now expected to be in British hands by the evening. Even greater news came through on the British Forces radio. "Germany has surrendered." Wow! Is it true? We will all be going home soon. I bet England is going mad now. Here we are in a very small post unknown to the outside world — "Kyauru" on a Burma beach celebrating VE Day with a bottle of Pussers Rum.

We were all very excited, but wondering what was going to happen to us now. Do you think we will have "a go" at the Japs at Singapore, or perhaps even invade Japan? Who knows? But I think it would be a hell of a fight to land troops in Japan.

On VE Day + 1 we worked until 10 o'clock when we spliced the main brace (two rums), slept all the afternoon and then spent the rest of the day writing letters home and then "whooping it up" on the beach fuelled by gin and rum. The date was 9th May 1945.

The next morning we felt deadly and spent the rest of the day in bed. The following morning, feeling refreshed, we set sail for Akyab at 5.30 a.m. and arrived in the afternoon to beach and load up with Royal Marines. The next day we arrived and unloaded the Marines. We guessed a big push from these parts would take place very soon, for over the past week or so there was a great build-up of equipment and troops, but we were not going to be part of it — we had been told we were going to Trincomalee that night.

We left our anchorage about 6 o'clock — no escort this time, so we made good progress and made Trinco in six days. It was quite an uneventful trip — we passed a school of whales, about four of them, playing, jumping and diving. It helped to break the monotony. On the sixth day we tied up in Trinco harbour, next to LSE1 — that means engineering ship. If parts had to be made, there was the equipment and the know-how on board an LSE for our use.

The engineer officer who was on LSE1 was Lt Joe Hinchly — he used to be our Lieutenant when we were in the Med the previous year. We had a good chat and wished each other well and we had a small whisky together in his cabin — not a bad bloke.

We sailed again early next morning, had a bit of fun and target practice — a plane towing a target made a series of runs over us and also a speedboat pulling a target roared past. As I was only an engine room grease monkey, I could only stand and watch in case I shot down the target plane. Never mind, they did let me have a go with a service revolver, shooting at a stationary target fixed to the midship guard rail.

Later in the day, the sky became very dark and we were warned that a storm was blowing up. By nightfall the wind was blowing force seven and eight and I thanked the Lord that the LCI was not now fixed to the upper deck like a limpet. The storm went on and on for about five hours and all the crew was on stand-by.

We in the engine room had to be vigilant, for if we lost power I'm sure we would have gone over. The engines were screeching every time the screws came out of the "oggin" and the rotor would be stifled as she crashed back down, just to start the procedure again. The storm blew itself out by about 5.00p.m. and everything seemed quiet and peaceful, but the upper deck looked a bit of a shambles. There were bits and pieces and parts of guard rails and tops of our ducts, etc. scattered everywhere. We had all been through a nightmare, but somehow there was an air of wonderment, or should I say sadness, all over the ship. "What's up?" I said to Jack Prince, a seaman Petty Officer, "Haven't you heard?" he replied, "Young Hobbs cannot be found."

There was really a feeling of sadness about the ship. Just to think, we had been all through the war in three continents without meeting death on board and now that all the wars were coming to an end we had to lose a young lad. Norman Hobbs was a nice, quiet, young seaman and had been part of our crew for about eighteen months. He was well liked and I can never remember him getting into trouble. There was the mystery over how he was lost. No one who worked with him could remember what he had been doing. Chief PO Cox could not give an explanation, but one of his mates did say that Chief Cox who was up on the fo'c'sle, phoned Hobbs and asked for him to meet him on the fo'c'sle. The weather at the time was atrocious and I can't imagine a Chief asking anyone to walk the length of the deck up to the bows in the middle of the night in a storm that was raging at that time. I did notice that a portion of the port guard rail was missing the next day.

As I was not involved in this tragedy, I never did hear if there was an outcome to this mystery. My opinion and also most of the crew thought it was very bad luck. Norman must have gone over the side with the guard rail that was missing. The skipper laid on a short service and said a few words, and the leading hand of his mess collected his naval bits and pieces and some personal possessions and raffled them. The skipper sent the proceeds to his parents. Life carried on as usual and it wasn't long before the whole episode faded, except of course for his close friends and family.

We were only in Trinco a couple of days before it was "up anchor" and off we go back into the wet monsoon weather — making for Bombay again. Life went on as usual and eventually we arrived back at Cochin, stopped for two days and then proceeded onwards to Bombay — we moved straight into the docks and tied up alongside. It looked as though we might be there for a little while for the Japs in the area seemed to be quiet, their headlong rush into India having been brought to a halt. It seemed that the forgotten Burma army, the Chindits, Royal Marines and the Gurkhas held fast and turned the Japs around, for they seemed to be on the run in most places. Also in the background, rumours of the "wonder bomb" or atom bomb, which everyone said would never be dropped, was lurking in everyone's minds.

The first watch went on a fortnight's leave — I was amongst that lot. Now, where shall I go? Weymouth, Paris, London? No, I'll just have to hang around the ship and try to keep out of trouble, not least because it was still raining! I went ashore to the Wayside Inn, then to the pictures, bored stiff all day. The next day I played football and we beat RN Headquarters team 7-0. What about that, then! I went to the pictures every other day, one ENSA concert and one ENSA show, "Gaslight", together with drinking and singing. That was about it — my holiday leave was over. It did appear we would be in Bombay for several weeks now, so our Sports Committee arranged several football and cricket matches with other ships and service establishments. We were now all trying to keep fit, cutting down on the fags, and doing a bit of jogging early mornings.

Life went on like this until America dropped the bomb on Hiroshima, and then Nagasaki — mass destruction and death in Japan. I don't know if we felt pleased or shocked — we of course were "over the moon" until all the horror stories started to be told, for it was now certain that we would be home and free within a thinkable time.

It was a day or so before Japan surrendered. First they asked for terms, and for two days reports came in but we were still kept waiting. Then, on 15th August, 1945, the great day was announced — headlines and radios screamed out "Japan surrenders". Of course, all work stopped and bottles were opened and the next day the "main brace" was well and truly spliced. The world had gone mad and we carried Fred back to the 406 out to the world.

What Now?

It took weeks rather than days to come back down to earth, and it seemed on looking back that our minds turned to "livestock" rather than shells and bombs. It started with some seamen who thought it was a good idea to bring back a monkey as an extra crew member. He was a lovely little chap (yes, he was a chap) and he was allowed the run of the upper deck. He wore a collar and was attached to a ship "throwing" line — I believe, these are about fifty feet long. He had plenty of rope and enjoyed climbing everywhere. Up ladders and down — into open doors and up and down stairs. Of course, what happened was that the rope would shorten every time he went round a post or ladder rung. After about half an hour or less, the rope would be only about one foot long and the poor little "sod" would jump and yell because he could hardly move. Then one of his "keepers" would have to untie the rope and untangle it from all the stairways ladders; that, of course, would take time.

I don't think the top brass approved of our new crew member and questions were asked like — who gave permission to buy the monkey, and did he go through joining routine like us? One morning Jacko was sitting on an inner guard rail looking at and picking around his belly — there were about six matelots laughing and pointing — Jacko had a "hard-on" and one of the lads was tickling him with a thin stick. That was the end of Jacko in the British Navy and he was sent ashore as soon as possible, no doubt to a good home — matelots are a soft lot.

The time had come to move into the inner harbour, and as I was on leave I could sit back and watch. It was great standing on the upper deck as the 406 was shunted back and forth. I could imagine Les in the engine room with the telegraph bells ringing: 100 revs forward, 1,000 revs reverse, etc. Les would be sweating and cursing: "Wish they would make their bloody minds up."

Once they had settled their move and we were tied up, I decided to go ashore for a bit of shopping. I went with Cliff and had a really good day. We had a good spend-up as I had to think about the near future. We could be going home within six months and no doubt Jen and I would be getting married. I reckon I must start getting some "rabbits" together for the great day.

Cliff and I started out looking in an open market. I bought a wristwatch, which turned out to be a good buy. Jen was delighted with it and I can tell you she still has it today, sixty years later! I also bought two sets of "jamas", two pairs of stockings, and two bedroom rugs for Mum. The shops would pack them up and send them home for you. I also ordered a pair of shoes to be made of snakeskin and white soft leather — these were to be made by a side-street shoemaker from our design and a cardboard cut-out size of Jen's foot — sent to me by post. The shoes turned out to be smashing — not another pair in England like them, and Jen was married in them.

After all this walking and buying, Cliff and I had a fish dinner in an up-market hotel and a couple of iced gin and tonics. A good day's shopping was had by all!

It seems the minds on board were still on livestock, for the Chief Chef had an idea to buy turkeys for Christmas dinner. This, of course, was discussed with all concerned and all who had to agree. The upshot was that it was agreed to buy some young turkeys and bring them on, for at this time no one would know where we would be at Christmas. It was now about three months away and this would give Chief Chef time to purchase about 15 turkeys and to arrange where they were going to be kept. After much arguing, it was decided that they could be kept in the space under the 12-pound cannon — a roll of wire could be bought and when the time came it would be rolled around the base of the gun platform to make a cosy little compound — that's if no one decided to fire the cannon. All this was agreed, so we had something to look forward to for the next few months, for we wouldn't purchase them until the beginning of November — I wonder if the war strategy was worked out as well as this!

We had been in Bombay a few weeks now and spent most of our time working on various bits and pieces, and also sorted out our motor whaler and the speed boat — both had been playing up just lately. Then on

Saturday 15th September I had to go into Headquarters in Bombay and meet an Engineer Commander who discussed my work and experience on the 406. He asked me about my previous experience in engineering, and also what I was going to do when I left the Navy. He said that as I had three years' deep sea time on ships' engines, I could sit for a deep sea certificate which would give me the chance for a good job ashore — especially in civil engineering. In my "wisdom" I turned him down by thanking him, explaining that I wanted to go back home and become a motor mechanic (big deal, he must have thought). Before he dismissed me he said that I had passed and I was promoted to the dizzy heights of an Acting Chief Motor Mechanic.

Five days later was my twenty-second birthday, so it was the usual sippers all round from the engineering crew — I honestly only had very small "sippers" and not one "gulper", but even then I passed out and woke up the next morning feeling deadly, which lasted all day.

Now that we had been "dock bound" for several weeks, the city had almost become our second home town. The Sports Committee had arranged plenty of football matches for us, but we had to forget cricket, owing to the monsoon and heavy rain. We went to the pictures in the city and aboard ship at least once a week and sometimes twice. The year was slipping by now and the wet weather did seem to be moderating, although one or two sunny and hot days were breaking out. We were soon to move out of Bombay in a day or so and make for Madras, a town we had not been ashore in. We heard that we were to pick up some troops and take them to Singapore. It was beginning to feel that we had been wasting our time hanging around India these last four months.

The Chief Chef had by now heard that the turkey chicks were big enough to bring aboard and could be picked up as soon as required. This suited us well as we would be calling into Madras on our way back to Singapore. The weather had again deteriorated when we reached our destination amid heavy rain and a choppy sea. We docked alongside and the crates of turkeys were soon aboard in their new home beneath the 12-pound gun ringed by wire mesh.

The birds settled down and were soon gobbling their food and grain which their seaman keepers obtained from their previous owners. Every time someone passed these new quarters they would look into the turkeys and say, "Gobble-gobble" and the turkeys would gather around and answer back, "gobble-gobble." Sometimes, when a different noise would frighten the birds, they would all flutter together and one or two would scuffle and jump up and try to fly over the wire mesh. There would always be one that could manage it and that one would end up perching on the guard rail swaying with the ship's movement. Then the bird would wobble, fall off its perch and float gently down into the blue "oggin". The seamen in charge would panic and shout "Turkey overboard, launch the whaler!" The ship would come to an abrupt halt and the whaler crew would soon lift the bird gently out of the sea — rescue accomplished. After all, it was their Christmas dinner that they had saved!

We had one more day in Madras before loading up with RAF personnel and Indian troops. We now had to make full speed to Singapore if we wanted our turkey dinner in harbour — at sea the celebrations would be seriously hampered. As the days went by it was obvious that we would still be at sea on Christmas Day and this was made certain when the port main engine broke down with a cylinder head blowing water from the cylinder liner seal at about 1400 hours, Christmas Eve.

We started work straight away, removing the number six cylinder head and had the engine running again by 2300 hours — full steam ahead again for Singapore and our turkey dinners. We then disappeared into the Engineer's cabin at his invitation, of course, until four o'clock in the morning, drinking his whisky. The last couple of days had also been hard work for the Chief Chef, for he and his boys and several helpers made up of seamen and stokers were busy despatching and plucking the turkeys. Of course, Christmas Day was now well and truly upon us, and it was agreed by all that Christmas dinner would be late this year, so we all sat down in our respective messes to devour a well-cooked turkey dinner with all the trimmings. The RAF and Indian Army boys on board catered for themselves and no doubt had their own festivities when they arrived at their own establishments.

In the evening we arranged a session of Housey Housey, or Bingo as it is now known, and it was good fun when played in a group of servicemen. It also helped to top up the mess funds. Although it was Christmas at sea, the boys did decorate their messes as usual. Our mess — the Engineers' PO mess — was really good. It was decorated with Japanese paper notes. Don't ask where they came from, but bearing in mind the Japanese were well and truly beaten, their money was now worthless. The notes were hung across and over the mess. There were larger notes, the size of foolscap paper, and medium and small notes in dozens of sizes and colours. There must have been thousands of pounds (or yen) hung across our dinner table and it was quite an eye-opener to realise that so much paper money could diminish to the value of paper decoration in the matter of a few days. This was a Christmas Day turning into a day to remember — broken down at sea, turkey dinner at sea and then back to life aboard a Royal Naval workhorse.

It was a further two days before we actually arrived in Singapore and tied up alongside a large oil tanker and, true to my days with Frank, I went aboard the tanker with Cliff and asked to meet the engineer officer. I went with Cliff because my old mate Frank Austin had left us before we sailed for India. I should have mentioned that before, because Frank and I became very good friends and I missed him and our talks very much.

The engineer aboard the tanker was true to his vocation. He made us welcome with a drop of the hard stuff and then gave us a conducted tour of his domain, to view his monster diesel engines. We were suitably impressed. The following day, after moving to the inner harbour to unload other RAF lads and the Indian Army, we went ashore to see what Singapore was all about. I was amazed how many Japanese were at work in the city, clearing, repairing and moving large boxes and pushing carts and wheelbarrows. This, of course, was a big city that had just fallen, and without a shot being fired.

There were hundreds of Japanese POWs in groups, being guarded by a few Brits and Aussies. The POWs were a motley lot — most of them were smaller than the average Brit, but there were lots of very tall men. I believe they were an élite guard regiment. What amused me was their footwear — it looked like leather gloves — each shoe had five pouches, one for each toe. They say these shoes were used by tree-climbers. They used to climb high trees and use this position as snipers.

We then had to move out of harbour and tie up alongside near Changi Jail. Changi had now become infamous for the horror dished out to the British and Aussie POWs. Hundreds of POWs were killed or tortured and beheaded by the Japanese, and where we were now docked we could see Japanese POWs digging up the bodies. Anyone visiting Changi now would not see it as it was then, for the land has been reclaimed from the sea and a new jail built, leaving a small part of the old one that was then used for religious services. This small port was left and was used as a museum to show the horrors that took place in this evil place.

Changi was a few miles by road from Singapore town and if we were to be docked here for any length of time it would be very difficult indeed to go into the town

152

without transport. Luckily, when we were in Madras the first time, it was noticed that a Ford 35-cwt truck was parked without a battery and looking very forlorn in the corner of some waste ground where we were docked. We made enquiries as to who owned the truck — as it was wartime it must have been part of the British Army at some time or other. As no one wanted it we, including the skipper, decided to garage it in the tank space of the 406, and we would make it roadworthy in our spare time. We were sure that the Army boys would help us out with parts if required. We were a scrounging lot! Anyway, everything went well with this old Ford truck and it was a godsend for the officers and men wherever we went.

Within a week we had another sailing to Madras, this time to pick up a regiment of Royal Marines and equipment. We were to be in Madras for at least three days, so our sports committee arranged a cricket match with an Army team stationed in Madras.

The day we were to sail was New Year's Day, and on the stroke of midnight all of the ships in the harbour and in the sound set off their whistles, horns, klaxons or what-have-you, in an ear-splitting noise of joy that the war was over.

In about eight days we pulled into Madras, this time to load up with rolling stock for the first time since we had rail lines fitted in the tank space. That evening a crowd of us went to the Sergeants' Mess at St George Fort — a very good time was had by all, with British beer flowing and of course all our old, and some new, songs were aired with great gusto.

153

The third day was the day our cricket match was arranged. It took place on a well-known ground where the national team played test matches against the MCC. We all went off in our Ford truck with our new kit and bag packed with everything a cricketer could think of — a brace of balls, wicket, bails and of course, the professional pads and gloves. I nearly forgot the brand-new spring-handled bats! Off we went, like pros, and we noticed how impressed the natives were when we asked the way to the ground. We pulled up eventually and swung open the imposing gates, proceeding down a drive to a parking lot next to a gleaming pavilion. We were aware of course, very early, that no one else had arrived. No doubt we were early because of our excitement.

We walked out onto the ground to inspect the wicket. There were about six. I wondered which one we could use and where the changing rooms were? We sat and lounged about waiting for our opponents, for they seemed to be very late — that was unusual for a grand place like this. In about three quarters of an hour of waiting, we became worried and were about to go and look around the pavilion, when all of a sudden a small Indian dressed in European clothes and straw hat shouted at us from the gate by the pavilion, waving his fists and hurrying towards us. "What you do here?" "Who are you?" "You must go quickly — you all trespass!" In the end he was almost overcome with rage and so beside himself that he could only shout in Hindi, and no one could understand anything. After much pushing and shoving he suddenly calmed down and it turned out we were at the wrong ground. This was only used for grand matches, much like Lords back home. Our match should have been held the other side of the town next to the railway sidings. For some reason it bore the same name as this: Royal Ground. This fracas came to an end with us humbly apologising and climbing into the back of our truck with our tails between our legs and muttering, "OK, sorry mate, no need to get on so — for Christ's sake pipe down."

By the time we were on our way again we were very late for our match, but we did get in a few overs before thirst stopped play. We had a good evening with the Army boys but I had to lay off the drinks because I was driving. In those days no one took much notice of drink-driving, although we had to watch it for I didn't want to lose my station card or breathing licence! Now that I was a chief motor mechanic, I had forgotten all about station cards.

The first week of the New Year went by without any earth-shattering news and we had all settled down to our new berth next to Changi. Dozens of Japanese POWs were sent on board to give the ship a good hose down and clean — they made a good job of it and we didn't have to torture and behead any of them! They all seemed to be well-behaved and well-mannered.

We had one more journey to Trinco, to transport several hundred Army boys and their equipment. Luckily the weather and sea conditions had now improved so the sailing back to Singapore was very smooth. We enjoyed a couple of good days in Trinco —

more shopping for the "coming wedding" and rabbits for the rest of them at home.

Before we sailed we spent three good hours swimming in the wonderful bay at Trinco. The sea was like blue glass and lukewarm. We fixed a rope on one of the boat's davits and had great fun swinging off them, letting go and smashing into the sea from about 25 feet. I reckoned we might miss this when we eventually tried to settle down in dear old England.

We sailed back to Singapore without mishap and dropped anchor in the sound, and then moved into our usual berth at Changi by the evening.

For the next few weeks life went on as usual: films on the upper deck every evening, and going into town to collect new films and provisions until one morning I was asked to drive a couple of the officers into town. I went to the usual place where the Ford was left and — wow! Our lovely Ford truck was missing. The whole ship's crew was devastated — all our freedom gone. Everyone, including the skipper, had a long face, but what could we do about it? It wasn't our truck anyway. The two officers I was going to drive into Singapore had to go by taxi — that would cost them. The next morning the sun was shining again and our beloved truck had been returned to its usual parking lot. We never did find out who carried out the dastardly deed.

The war had been over now for six months or so, and we were all on edge and wondering what was next. In fact I think we were all getting bored with no real work to do. Why doesn't someone mention those lovely words "Going home"? We were still working, moving the Army and their equipment but it seemed we were just filling in time by playing football or cricket and going into town for a few "wets" (booze!).

Then in the middle of February something happened that put the wind up us. The skipper cleared the lower deck for a talk on our next operations. It appeared that there was trouble brewing in Malaysia with Communists who had started sabotage and stirring up the locals. Several small skirmishes had broken out and the Army took a load of prisoners, but during the nights the temporary prisons were raided — men were set free by raiders. The skipper said that when we were part of the mission we were not allowed to write letters and were not to talk to anyone about the plan, and the number 406 had to be painted over. The plan was to beach the 406 for the Army to load the tank space with these Communist prisoners. This had to be hush-hush, for the men would be political prisoners and no one wanted to start upsetting the Asian countries — especially India, which at that time was a little bit shaky.

The next day we set sail from Singapore and made our way up the coast of Malaysia, beaching on the chosen beach as arranged. We were all hyped up now wondering what sort of men these prisoners would be. Would we have to watch them all the time, lock them up, or guard them with guns? Anyway, we arrived at the beach on time. It was still dark. We had an early breakfast and all the crew were ready for anything. Then we waited and waited. No prisoners, no nothing, no one did turn up, so eventually the whole political plan was called off, thank goodness, and we returned to our "home" — Changi, Singapore.

We never did hear about our mission with the Communist prisoners again. We were all pleased for we felt that if we did get embroiled in the politics of Malaysia we could be involved for many months and probably miss our return to Blighty. The only thing to be done now to put things right in our eyes was to repaint no. 406 on our bows. This, of course, was done in no time, for sailors are used to using the paintbrush.

Back in Changi everything was back to normal. The truck was taken into town twice that day to pick up the mail and provisions: fresh greens and eggs. The next day I drove our engineer officer into Singapore for further orders when he suddenly asked me if I wanted to leave the 406. I was gobsmacked. I didn't want to move to another ship as I was already near my demob number and if I moved to another ship it might mean I would move to another theatre of operation which might put my demob back a few months. I explained all this to him and said I had been happy and enjoyed my time on the 406 but, like most of us on board, I had had enough and more than anything just wanted to go home and carry on with my life married to Jen. So, my answer to his question was "yes", I did want to leave the 406, but on the other hand I would be very sorry to be leaving such a great crew and so many mates. It turned out there were plenty of "buzzes" going around that there would be lots of the original crew leaving very soon and we were advised to sort out our kit and start packing.

It was Friday 22nd March when I was informed that I was going on draft the next day. My kit was now all packed, my hammock that had been stowed away for years was brought out and unrolled, checked and again rolled in the correct manner, looking very tidy and easy to manage. I left the old 406 on Saturday 23rd March 1946, after shaking hands with those staying behind. It was eight o'clock in the morning as we loaded our kits into a tender, which took us across the water to the barracks and, as per RN rules, we had to go through the "joining and leaving routine".

We first joined the barracks, filled in all the forms, queued to see the doctor, queued to see the paymaster and kit issue boys, and then collected a station card (breathing licence). As we were leaving the next day we had to go through leaving routine. Believe it or not, the same regulators who had joined us that morning then turned in their chairs and faced the next window and proceeded to release us. All the same forms had to be filled in for leaving. We had been queuing all day and were almost "all in" before we returned the new station card for leaving. After all that, no breathing licence again. It was at least 1600 hrs before we had done with all the leaving and joining business, and then the new development was posted on the notice board. The names of all those drafted to the UK were to leave Singapore at 1600 hrs on LST 3021, and my name was there. Whoopee! It's all over at last.

Then I began to think. I had been on a flat-bottomed LST for almost 3½ years, and, with all the modern motor ships moored in Singapore harbour, I was to go home on a steam LST that would take six weeks! Mustn't grumble, we were going the right way and I guess it would be like a six-week holiday cruise, for I didn't know a thing about steam LSTs. Really, my story is told — at least it will be when I step ashore in England in six weeks' time.

We started our journey at 1600 hrs on Sunday and pulled into Trinco six days later to tie up alongside an oil tanker and take on fuel. We had by now settled in aboard our new abode, but I don't think any of us felt the pride we did when on the 406. It was more like a sea-going hotel than a Navy ship.

It turned out there was a lot of our old crew on board. There was Bill, Les, Fred and Raggy Rex and a couple of our officers, and at least four others from the seamen crew, so we had plenty of friends to go ashore with or just sit about and talk to.

We went ashore that first evening and had "Big Eats" in a good watering hole we had got to know when we pulled into Trinco with the 406. We stayed in Trinco another three days and had fun swimming over the side. It was getting hot again, so it was a chance to cool down.

We went to sea again the next day — our next stop would be Aden. It was eleven days before we steamed into Aden, which looked a barren place. We went ashore and really had an uproarious sort of day — maybe we thought it might be the last time we could really let our hair down.

Six of us started about 1000 hrs. There was Bill, Les, Fred, Raggy, Cliff and myself. We wandered into the town ready for anything. We started on coffee and sticky cakes and gin, and then somebody suggested we hire a horse and gharry, but the driver in white flowing robes would not let the six of us ride together. He jumped off his seat holding a long whip and went around the rear to make sure everyone aboard was seated. This was a chance for one, who shall remain nameless, to climb on the back of the horse, smack his behind like a cowboy shouting, "Gee up!" Of course off he galloped with us whooping in the back and the driver running behind waving his long whip shouting, "Stop, stop." At the end of the busy street we thought we had gone far enough. The horse slowed down and we all got out and waited for "Johnny", with his whip, to catch us up. We gave him a screwed-up ball of paper money and let him go with a pat on his head. I don't think he was very happy, and thinking back we must have been the start of the "yobbo" culture. Our excuse was that we had been partying most of the night and the "neaters" rum had not worn off.

The next hour or so we passed the time of day by walking, looking and trying to savour the atmosphere of such an ancient and mystic place (perhaps the rum was still working!). After a good meal of "goat" and very hot rich curry, we hired a couple of taxis to take us to the races, which were to be held that afternoon. Everything went according to plan and we all piled onto the racecourse. I forget how much it cost us, but I know we grumbled that we weren't made of money. However, we had a great afternoon and I remember I backed two firsts and one second, so I made enough to pay for my day out. The races were well presented although some of the horses were a bit past it, but there were some very good horses running and it looked as if there was plenty of money about.

After a few native brews we all piled into a couple of taxis and were taken to Greater Aden to buy a few things. I think my purchase was a comb. As it was now getting dark, the taxis were still waiting for us so we had a ride into the desert and across the border into Yemen (we were told later that this was very dangerous). The taxis took us to see good "shows" which turned out to be "very blue", but it could have turned nasty so we told the taxis to take us back to Aden as soon as possible. They agreed if we paid more money. This we had to do for we were across the border and could have been kidnapped or arrested. Anyway, we were enjoying a good day out, it was peacetime and we were on our way home. No more adventures like this again.

The next morning we were all very fragile. I just about ate my toast and poached egg, and a strong cup of tea, and felt a bit better, but Fred and Bill were missing. Still, we had "make and mend" all day and we were to stay in Aden until tomorrow so we just had to keep out of the way and out of sight. Later on in the evening the six of us met up again and discussed our day out in Aden and we all agreed it was "a good run ashore", especially the afternoon at the races. What about the cowboy act riding bareback down the high street? We were all ashamed over this so early in the morning. It wouldn't have been so bad if it had been at turning-out time!

162

We had now been told that we would be sailing the next afternoon, first stop Suez. This should take about seven days. It was 1800 hrs when we steamed out of Aden. The weather was blowing enough to cause a choppy sea, and as we were still a bit fragile we kept out of the way and slept it off. It took us six days to reach the Suez Canal and we went ashore in Port Said at about 1800 hrs.

It was cold in Port Said, so we all donned our Blues. There were plenty of bumboats alongside as usual, but the "rubbish" was too dear to buy so we gave it a miss this time.

The weather had turned very cold for the Med as we set off full steam ahead for Gibraltar. We forecast it would take us about eight or nine days at the rate we had been going. This steam LST was not bad but not as quick as the old 406, but we did make it in the morning of the ninth day despite some very bad weather and heavy rolling.

We arrived at Gibraltar at about 2100 hrs, and just about had time to go ashore to the RN canteen for some English beer. It was a welcome change and we had a good time with several of our old crew, that was until a yank started kicking the chair next to where I was sitting. He was getting on my nerves so I picked the chair up and bumped it down away from him. He gave me a look but said nothing. I forgot all about this incident until I stood up and went through the door to go outside. The yank was standing behind the door and took a swing at me as I went by. Fortunately he missed and just knocked my cap off, and before I knew what was happening three of my "oppos" jumped him and slung him through the door (good mates to have!). That was the last we saw of him, so it was drinks all round again. We had a good run ashore that evening and managed to keep trouble at arm's length.

It was ashore again the next morning, so I went to the bank and drew out some money, buying myself a watch and also some dress material for Mum. All this helped to fill up my "rabbit bag".

We sailed out of Gibraltar for the last time on Friday 3rd May. The weather was bad and LST 3021 was rolling heavily. In fact, the rolling continued for the next four days and didn't improve until just before we entered the English Channel. The sun came out and the sea improved just like magic as we pulled into Plymouth during the morning of Thursday 9th May 1946.

We left the ship to travel to RN barracks Chatham almost immediately, arriving late morning. Guess what happened next? We started joining routine once again and had to queue all day as we went from office to office, but this time we had to queue for our leave chits and rail tickets. We were home in England but we missed our dinner and also our leave that evening.

In the morning I was free to go home and plan the rest of my life with Jennifer. There was one thing that I thanked God for: all of my family and Jennie's were alive and in good health after the greatest war known to man, which in some way we all took part in.

Postscript

I duly married Jennie, my long-time sweetheart, on 22nd June 1946. I returned to Skurray's, one year even being Vauxhall's Manager of the Year. I worked there for the next 30-odd years before Jennie and I, along with my brother Brian, ran our own vehicle insurance assessor's business.

Our daughter Pauline was born on 11th February 1947. She married Bill Campbell on 30th March 1968, presenting us with two granddaughters, Sarah and Tracey. Sarah and Darren have children of their own, Lewis and Ryan, and so we are great-grandparents now! Tracey is to marry Jeff next year, so more celebrations lie ahead.

Jennie has written a few pages of her early life, which will be of particular interest for friends and family.

I hope you have enjoyed reading this as much as I have enjoyed writing it. If not, be warned . . . I may have to put pen to paper again one day!

Appendix — My Early Years, by Jennie

I was born on 30th November 1925, the first child to Albert William Thomas Ilett and Florence Caroline Ilett née Clarke — Bill and Flo to everyone. My mother's father died before she was born and so Mum never knew him. As there were no widow's pensions in those days, her mother had to work, which must have been very difficult trying to raise a family of five children. One of the boys, Will, died of consumption (TB) at the age of 18, and the only other thing I know is that her mother lived her final years in Devizes Asylum. The poor lady clearly had a very difficult life. The only recollection I have of her was when I was about three years old. All I remember is that she wore a long skirt and apron and that she was quite tall . . . but then again, anyone would be to a three-year-old!

My father's mother was Sarah Mariah Minnie Louise Bull . . . so she must have been delighted to have changed her surname when she married William Albert John Ilett. They both hailed from London, Gran from

Pentonville (outside the prison, I hasten to add). Gramp came from just down the road in Islington.

Dad was the oldest of six children, the others all being girls — Ethel, May, Rose, Doris and Adeline (Addy). These aunts were virtually like sisters to me as I grew up, Addy being only ten years my senior. I was bridesmaid to Addy; the other sisters I remember getting married were May and Rose.

My brother John was born when I was four, and we lived at 53 Wellington Street in New Swindon. The house was on three levels, and I remember Mum taking me to the top floor to see the R101 airship flying overhead. This was very exciting at a time when nothing else apart from birds was ever seen in the skies. Sadly, shortly afterwards, the R101 crashed and exploded in France killing 44 of the 52 people on board.

The year after John was born, my parents were in the fortunate position of being able to buy a house in Oxford Road, Stratton St Margaret, something which was quite unusual before the war. The house was called St Michael . . . nothing to do with Marks and Spencer! My grandparents also bought a house in Oxford Road at this time — their house was called Redhill. Both houses were three-bedroom semis.

Upstairs, along with the bedrooms, was a bathroom with hot running water, which was a pleasant change after Wellington Street when I had to have a bath in front of the fire, the tin bath being brought in from the back yard and filled with buckets of hot water from the brick copper which lived in the scullery. The new house also had an indoor toilet, which was far preferable to getting cold outside or having to use a chamber pot at night. However, even with a posh indoor loo, we still had to cut up newspaper to hang on a piece of string!

St Michael had a very long back garden, in which Dad could indulge his love of gardening. Along with most others at this time, we grew our own vegetables; we also had blackcurrants, blackberries, gooseberries, raspberries and strawberries, along with apple, pear and plum trees. Needless to say, we always had a good supply of jam and bottled plums. I also recall copious amounts of rhubarb, and Dad had a greenhouse for his tomatoes, so all in all we were pretty self-sufficient.

One year Dad bought a lawnmower, which caused great excitement. It was hard work as it had to be pushed, and was a very heavy contraption despite being only about 12 inches wide, but at the time it was the height of sophistication. Dad also had a cine camera, which was quite rare, and we have reams of film of us all trying out the lawnmower — such simple delights in an uncomplicated world.

Dad also had a shed in which he would potter about, no doubt happy to get away from his noisy children. There was a "last" in the shed, on which he mended our shoes. One year Dad had the bright idea of buying half-a-dozen ducks at the market. He proudly left them in a tin bath overnight, only to be shocked to find them all dead in the morning. They could not get out and had drowned. We never had ducks again.

Dad rode a motorbike, and an abiding memory is seeing Gramp riding along in the open sidecar wearing his cap, woollen scarf, wire-rimmed glasses, and with

169

his coat wrapped tightly round as he happily read his paper, probably The Evening Advertiser, as they went to work. Gramp also had a kiss curl in the middle of his forehead, which sprang back whenever I pulled it. Virtually everyone in Swindon worked for The Great Western Railway. The other big employer in the area was Wills, the cigarette manufacturer; women mostly worked there.

Dad was a fitter and turner in the Locomotive Department of The GWR, working with the erectors who built the steam engines. Gramp worked there on a lathe, which is no doubt how Dad got his job. Both of them worked nights for almost all of their careers. Of course my grandfather had worked on the Gold Coast of West Africa in his earlier years. The GWR ran such good apprenticeships that their engineers were in demand all over the world.

Uncle Jim worked in Kenya for several years for the Crown Agents prior to the Mau Mau uprising. In fact, Gordon and I were planning on going out to join him in Kenya shortly after we were married. We had completed all the paperwork and were just making the final arrangements when we heard that the position had been taken by someone else — wheels within wheels! We were bitterly disappointed at the time, but I am getting ahead of myself so will return to my childhood years.

My schooldays began in 1930. I suppose I was just an average pupil, always coming about midway in the exams. My interest was more in sports and athletics than the three Rs. I enjoyed hockey and netball, and training for the high jump and running. I even managed to get to Loughborough College to run for Wiltshire.

After the school sports day we broke up for the long summer holiday. John and I and our friends roamed the fields at the back of our houses with sandwiches (probably jam!) and bottles of water. We were lucky the day the "pop man" called as we were allowed to take a bottle of Tizer with us as a treat to share. Those days the sun always seemed to be shining.

The whole of the Great Western Railway factory shut down for Trip Week, the first week in July. Consequently the schools broke up then, otherwise there would have been no children at school because GWR employed 80 per cent of the workers in Swindon. There was no pay for the workers during Trip Week, but special trains were laid on and passes were provided, so no one had to pay.

Families who could not afford to have the whole week away would go down to Weston-super-Mare on what was known as Trip Wednesday — they just spent the day there before going back home. We were more fortunate, and for our week had a choice of destinations. We usually went to St Ives or Newquay — other favourite resorts were Great Yarmouth and Weymouth. One year we even went to Jersey, no doubt getting a free pass on the GWR ferry!

It was always exciting looking forward to our holiday, and I remember my mother packing a big trunk a week before with all the clothes for the family. This was then collected by a great big GWR lorry and sent off to our destination. It was then a case of waiting as the time dragged until it came to the day for going on holiday!

We walked the three or four miles to the station in the evening to board the train in the sidings. As they were special trains there wasn't a platform, so my father would get a ladder from somewhere so that my grandparents, several aunts, my mother, brother and finally myself could get up into the carriage.

So off we went late at night, arriving the following morning. When we were going to Cornwall, the train took us along the coast just as it was getting light — we even seemed to be running along the beach at Dawlish. When we arrived in St Ives, the landladies were there to meet us, taking us to the fishing cottages where we were to spend the week. My mother did the shopping for food and gave it to our landlady, Mrs Ninnes.

Mrs Ninnes and her husband Sam were a lifeboat family in St Ives; indeed, whenever you see photos of lifeboats in that area, almost everyone seems to be named Ninnes. Sam would walk up and down the quay all day, along with his pals — this would stem from the time when they were at sea and could only walk up and down the deck for exercise.

The first day on Trip Week we would go down to the beach and hire a tent. We never organised things specifically, but invariably we would find ourselves next to our neighbours — in fact it was just like Oxford Road. This also meant that the families would get together to celebrate any of the children's birthdays which occurred during our stay.

We used to have two tents, because my grandparents and the wider family came with us. We would play on the beach for most of the holiday, weather permitting, although I always remember it being excellent. We might also go to an art display, as St Ives was famous for this.

There were two beaches in St Ives, one being warm and one being cold, depending which coastline they were on — obviously we always went to the warm one! I also recall seeing the fish being landed on the quay and being sold to the traders.

Towards the end of the morning, Mum would pop off and get some rolls for lunch, which would be consumed with great relish after all our exercise swimming in the sea and playing games with our friends on the beach. Virtually the whole holiday would be spent this way, and wonderful times they were. I particularly remember the delicious ice cream being made with real Cornish clotted cream.

One receipt I have from these times shows that my parents paid £5 to Mrs Ninnes, which covered the board for the four of us. This may not sound like much money today, but I expect that my parents would have had to save for it in a holiday club so that we could afford our time away.

I do know that my parents paid one shilling (5p after decimalisation) a week into The Great Western Medical Fund so that we had free treatment if this were ever needed. Of course, it must be remembered that the National Health Service did not come into being until 1948; prior to this, all treatment and doctors' bills had to be paid for by the patient — if you couldn't pay, you didn't receive any treatment. This scheme was so good that Aneurin Bevan used it as a blueprint for the NHS.

The Great Western Railway was a wonderful company and looked after us well. They even had a hospital we could use. I don't recall that we were a particularly unhealthy family, although John did break some bones in his foot when he climbed onto the cast iron mangle and it fell on him — boys will be boys!

Mum used to go to Mason's, a fairly high-class grocer's . . . for Swindon, at least! There were chairs at the counter for the customers to sit down while they were being served . . . well, for the grown-ups. Mason's sold everything from cooked meats to biscuits in tins at the front of the counter. They were sold loose, with the broken ones being cheaper. Sugar came in sacks and tea in tea-chests, both being weighed into the required quantities. The sugar was weighed into blue bags, as was dried fruit, and the assistants were very adept at folding the tops to ensure that everything was carefully sealed — whenever I tried, it never worked! Butter came in blocks and would be patted into half-pound pats. I was always amazed at how they could cut precisely half a pound from the huge block. And, of course, the butter would be stamped with the maker's brand, be it a thistle or a swan.

Mason's had a wonderful smell, no doubt due to their vast diversity of goods, be it vinegar, which was poured into the bottle you supplied, bacon, sliced so expertly, or the wonderful cakes bought by the slab. Actually, I used to buy our vinegar from Pope's, the corner shop on Oxford Road, which was more convenient. Mrs Pope was an old lady who wore her hair in a bun. She was a bit of a tartar so there was no chance of taking any liberties. She used to take the bottle to a barrel of vinegar at the back of the shop, and my treat on the way home was to take a swig before giving the bottle back to Mum.

Ansty's, a draper's in Regent Street, was an Aladdin's cave as far as I was concerned, as was McIlroy's, the department store next door, which was even bigger and where the apprentices lived above the shop. McIlroy's also had tearooms and a ballroom. In fact, our daughter Pauline was later so see the Beatles there . . . but again I am getting ahead of myself.

Much of our food was delivered, the butcher, baker and greengrocer all having delivery boys; however my favourite was the "Walsey Man", the Walls ice cream man with his "Stop me and buy one" tricycle from which we would buy our Snofrutes if we had been good. There was also the muffin man with his bell and carrying his wares on a tray on his head. On Sunday there was even a man coming round selling watercress. Milk was delivered by Mr Dunn in his horse and cart carrying the churns into which were dipped the different sized ladles to pour into the jugs we supplied. As we had our own chickens in the garden, we rarely required eggs. Fortunately, the chickens fared better than the ducks!

Our coal was delivered by the GWR, Mum being careful to count the number of sacks as it was not unknown to be charged for ten bags and only nine being emptied into the wooden coal bunker at the side of the house. The only foolproof method was to count the number of empty sacks as the coal was deposited.

The first time I ever met Gordon Turner was at the County Ground, a park where Barbara, Audrey and I used to wander — we were 15, having left school the previous year. Gordon used to play football and cricket at the County Ground, but on this occasion he was waiting to be picked up to play at a dance in Shrivenham as he was in a dance band. I remember that he was sitting on his trumpet case, but I cannot say that he made much of an impression on me.

A few weeks later I was roller-skating at Swindon baths, needless to say at the Great Western building. In the winter the baths were covered over and part was used for roller-skating. Gordon swept me off my feet — literally. He crashed right into me, knocking me clean off my feet. He was apologetic afterwards and seemed fairly concerned. He even offered to walk me home, but when I told him where I lived, he changed his mind and I ended up catching the bus home with Barbara.

I suppose he couldn't have been too bad because we had arranged to meet to go to the pictures. We went as a foursome with Barbara and Ken Morgan to the Arcadia in Regent Street to see one of the "Road" films with Bob Hope, Bing Crosby and Dorothy Lamour. In the film there was a fire on an island, and strangely enough we could smell burning. There was burning — it was Gordon's new coat! He had put it under his seat, and there must have been a smouldering cigarette because his coat was smoking and the manager appeared with a bucket of water. Gordon's new coat emerged soaking, which made it all the worse when we came out of the cinema to find it snowing.

Gordon was working at Skurray's Garage as an apprentice mechanic, but he'd taken the day off because he had just had a smallpox vaccination and was told that he could have time off if he wasn't feeling well. As it happened, he did look a bit white after we had been passed by a posh car. He turned round and swore, saying that his boss was in the car and that he would be in trouble!

Apparently, Ken was also interested in me and so there was a bit of awkwardness between him and Gordon. Gordon tells me that they eventually tossed a coin for me . . . and Gordon reckons he lost!

Also available in ISIS Large Print:

Bow and Arrow War

Marjorie Inkster

"Our hands were red and swollen with chilblains and we all had terrible colds and coughs, but we were extraordinarily happy."

This is the story of a 19-year-old who joined the FANY then trained as a radar mechanic during the 1939–45 war. From 1943 Marjorie Inkster was a radar maintenance officer on London gunsites, including Hampstead, Primrose Hill and Mill Hill. The work entailed taking responsibility for a group of REME craftsmen and NCOs. Full of lively descriptions of daily work practises, gun sites and the people working on them, air-raids, the Officers' Mess and the fast development of army radar, this is an interesting look at life as an FANY. Also there is praise for the Royal Electrical and Mechanical Engineers, without whom no guns could have fired in our defence.

ISBN 978-0-7531-9498-0 (hb)
ISBN 978-0-7531-9499-7 (pb)

On and Off the Flight Deck

Henry "Hank" Adlam

"We had seen enough now to know that we would be lucky, either one of us, to see the end of the war and the future was always a taboo subject with any of us."

Hank Adlam began his naval flying career in January 1941 when he entered the flying course at Gosport naval barracks. Subsequently, on completion of flying training at Netheravon, he was selected as a fighter pilot and moved to the fighter school at Yeovilton. He took part in operations against the enemy from two Escort Carriers and one Fleet Carrier in the Atlantic, Arctic, Mediterranean and Far Eastern theatres of war. He went on to fly in operations against the Japanese in 1945, helping with the American battle for Okinawa.

His book is not about heroes and leaders of naval air warfare, although he points out that there were many of them, but a portrayal of an average young man, anxious to fight for his country, but having to cope with the tension of warfare.

ISBN 978-0-7531-9494-2 (hb)
ISBN 978-0-7531-9495-9 (pb)

The Flight of the Young Sparrow

Trudi Spatz

"No one spoke a word as we all had our own thoughts about the unknown future. Kurt and I looked out of the window, a last glance of Hamburg, and we wondered whether we would ever see Hamburg again."

This is the fascinating account of the experiences of Trudi Spatz in the turbulent years before, during and after the Second World War. Brought up as a young girl in Nazi Germany, she and her family managed to escape to England in 1938 after her father fell foul of the authorities. Her memoir charts the family's struggle for survival and the many trials and tribulations they faced whilst trying to live as "free" citizens in wartime England.

Eventually, Trudi was called up for service and embarked on a new phase in her life. She found herself undertaking a series of varied jobs, eventually reaching her longed-for goal — to become a teacher.

ISBN 978-0-7531-9488-1 (hb)
ISBN 978-0-7531-9489-8 (pb)

Bugle Boy

Len Chester

"Sleeping on a straw-filled palliasse was like lying on the back of a hedgehog. But nothing had prepared me for day one."

From the day he went to his elder brother's Kings' Squad Parade at Chatham in 1937, all Len Chester wanted was to become a bugler/drummer boy. Two years later, when he was 14, he did just that and joined the Royal Marines.

He tells of life on board HMS Iron Duke in the dangerous waters of Scapa Flow and then on the Arctic convoys to Russia, how he learned the many bugle calls, and of playing at the funerals of men when he had never been to a funeral before. Len Chester survived the war and came home. At Remembrance Day parades he wears the rare off-white beret to which only men from the Arctic Convoys are entitled — yellow-white because blood turns yellow when frozen in snow.

ISBN 978-0-7531-9486-7 (hb)
ISBN 978-0-7531-9487-4 (pb)